CHINA STUDIES SERIES

ECONOMIC CHANGES IN RURAL CHINA

By Luo Hanxian

Translated by
Wang Huimin

NEW WORLD PRESS
Beijing, China

First Edition   1985

Cover design by Sun Chengwu

HN
740
.Z9
C64613
1985

ISBN 0-8351-1525-9

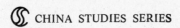 CHINA STUDIES SERIES

Published by
NEW WORLD PRESS
24 Baiwanzhuang Road, Beijing, China

Printed by
FOREIGN LANGUAGES PRINTING HOUSE
19 West Chegongzhuang Road, Beijing, China

Distributed by
CHINA INTERNATIONAL BOOK TRADING CORPORATION
(GUOJI SHUDIAN)
P.O. BOX 399, Beijing, China

Printed in the People's Republic of China

CONTENTS

LIST OF TABLES

PREFACE

In 1983, the New World Press published *Chinese Village Close-up*, a collection of my investigative reports on Kaixian'-gong Village, as part of their "China Studies Series". The book is called *Close-up* because it records a number of visits I made to Kaixian'gong over the course of nearly half a century, and the changes that have taken place there during this time. Actually, this small village, with its population of 2,000, represents merely a single tree in China's vast forest of one billion people. One may rightly ask: Are the nearly one million large and small rural villages in China all like Kaixian'gong? Isn't this a case of "not seeing the forest for the trees"? The answer to this question is both yes and no.

On the one hand, many villages in China are identical to Kaixian'gong, in that they were formed under similar historical conditions and for 2,000 years have been component parts of a unified and centralized administrative structure. Their identical essential nature and outward appearance makes it possible to reveal the general character of all Chinese villages by means of a thorough and detailed investigation and analysis of any one village. We must consider, however, the vast territory occupied by the Chinese people — an area bordering on frigid Siberia in the north, stretching nearly to the equator in the south with the islands of the South China Sea, extending west to the Pamir and Himalaya Mountains, and fronted on the east by the Pacific Ocean. No other country possesses such a wide range of climatic and geographical differences. Those who inhabit this vast land adapt their production and life style to the particular conditions prevalent where they live. Moreover, the Chinese nation is composed of more than 50 nationalities which have long traditions of mutual intercourse. Although these groups live in close harmony, historical circumstances have resulted in differ-

7

ences in language, culture, customs and even social structure; together they present a picture of great diversity within unity, though regional differences exist within individual nationalities. Each and every village in China has its own individual character, with the differences manifesting themselves mainly in terms of degree. For the above reasons, then, the description of Kaixian'gong Village in *Chinese Village Close-up* cannot be applied to all villages in China.

The dual nature of the answer given above leads us to the following conclusion: If a non-Chinese reader is not to end up with a one-sided view of the subject as presented in *Chinese Village Close-up*, he or she must consult a more general work on the Chinese countryside. It is for this reason that I am particularly grateful to the New World Press for having assigned Luo Hanxian with the task of writing *Economic Changes in Rural China*, and for publishing it alongside *Chinese Village Close-up* in the "China Studies Series".

Luo Hanxian and I have been friends and colleagues for more than 40 years. During the War of Resistance Against Japan (1937-1945) we participated in the democratic movement in the Southwest of China and were active in the China Democratic League. Recognizing the important role played by the peasantry in Chinese society, economy and politics, the two of us made this the subject of our research. At the same time, though we held many views in common regarding the solution of China's peasant problems, we also had our differences.

Luo Hanxian's research dealt with the peasant economy from the point of view of political economy, while my field of specialization was sociology and social anthropology. This naturally led to our practicing different research methods. Stated simply, Luo observed the changes taking place in the Chinese countryside from macroscopic perspective, while I approached the subject in a more anatomical, microscopic way. Were we both to remain within the confines of our respective disciplines, there would be little need for scholarly exchange. But as for researching the actual reforms in and development of the Chinese countryside, an endeavor requiring both broad and penetrating understanding, cooperation between our two disciplines is indispensable.

My choice, over the course of nearly half a century, of social anthropology as a methodology by which to study the Chinese peasantry was inspired by both subjective reasons and objective conditions. The former I have set forth in my preface to *Earthbound China*, published in the 1950s. In that book I expressed dissatisfaction with the research methods in vogue at the time, which on the one hand presented numerous statistics but lacked a theoretical foundation, and on the other failed to make use of locally compiled information while blindly copying conclusions obtained from non-Chinese sources. This led to my suggestion that scholars engaged in investigating the Chinese countryside go to the countryside and do their fieldwork there. To this day I still maintain that this classical research method, originally advocated by Mao Zedong, is the ideal method for the study of human society. Mao, in fact, described it figuratively as "dissecting a sparrow".

Though we must continue to develop this method of investigation, it has become increasingly apparent that it has its limitations when applied across the vast spectrum of Chinese society. In the last few years, I have been striving to strike a balance between the macro- and microscopic approaches, between quantitative and qualitative analyses, and between theory and practice. During this time, it is Luo Hanxian who has been my greatest source of both inspiration and assistance. Several months ago, when Luo, myself and a number of scholars from various disciplines went to southern Jiangsu Province to study the small towns in the area, we attempted to integrate the above-mentioned balances into our work.

In defense of the classical method of research, I would like to mention some of the objective conditions under which it was developed in China. Looking back over the past 50 years, in the 1930s and 1940s, China was in the midst of a profound national crisis; in the early years after Liberation in 1949, the new People's Republic was confronted with the numerous tasks of national reconstruction, many of which could not be completed immediately. The following decades witnessed periods of "Leftist" disturbances during which it was nearly impossible to carry out normal scientific research, and my own research in the countryside was met with great resistance.

When I began my research as an anthropologist in the 1930s, I worked singlehandedly as an independent explorer. In 1936, after spending one short month in Kaixian'gong, I felt that this small village of only 2,000 people was a much larger field than I could handle. In the 1940s, some other young researchers and myself set up a small-scale social research center at Yunnan University, where we could choose from a variety of village types to carry out comparative research. As described in *Earthbound China*, we studied Lu Village, with its entire economy devoted to agriculture; Yi Village, with its well-developed handicrafts industry; and Yu Village, with its economy influenced by commercial ties with the nearby market town. Our plan was to make comparisons among these three villages and from this describe the general character and appearance of China's inland villages. But, due to limited manpower and finances, we were only able to carry out qualitative analyses; broad-based sampling and statistical analysis would have been impossible under those conditions.

In the mid-1950s, I set out to revisit those villages where work had previously been done, and plot the changes which had taken place in the social system. However, for various political reasons, this project had to be postponed until the present decade. The results of this survey appear in the final chapters of *Chinese Village Close-up*.

While carrying out this fieldwork in 1981, I became aware of the necessity of, and the potential for, expanding the scope of our research. This realization followed the fall of the Gang of Four and the correcting of "Leftist" errors in policy, whereupon the development of the social sciences in China assumed greater importance than any time since Liberation. After an absence of nearly 30 years, sociology courses were revived in the universities; the Chinese Academy of Social Sciences established a research institute of sociology; and several universities

reopened departments of sociology. With the support of the
Party and the entire country, investigation into the countryside
on a large-scale basis became a real possibility. At the same
time, correcting "Leftist" policies and instituting the production
responsibility system during the last five years has led to general prosperity throughout the Chinese countryside, accompanied
by rapid changes in the rural social and economic structure.
These altogether satisfactory changes are not only of the greatest
interest to scholars involved in studying the peasantry and the
countryside; they also provide those engaged in practical work
in the countryside with valuable material which must be examined in a realistic manner.

To follow the course of this objective development, it seems
more necessary than ever before to integrate the micro- and
macroscopic approaches and effect coordination among a wide
range of disciplines in studying China's rural problems. This
change away from the subjective is a reflection of the rapid and
large-scale changes taking place in the Chinese countryside today, and is sure to lead to a great broadening of and unprecedented achievements in this field of research. These wide-rang-
ing changes are the subject of the last two sections of the present book. They are serving not only to fire the enthusiasm of
the broad masses of Chinese peasants as they progress swiftly
down the road of socialism, but also to stimulate those scholars
studying the Chinese countryside and peasantry; boundless fertile fields await our cultivation and development.

                                                Fei Hsiao Tung
Beijing
January 2, 1984

Chapter I

INTRODUCTION

The juncture of the 1940s and 1950s marked the beginning of fundamental changes in Chinese history. Before the founding of the People's Republic in 1949, China was a semi-feudal and semi-colonial society. The feudal society that preceded it had lasted for thousands of years. Of the numerous explanations investigators have advanced for this phenomenon, one that has been generally acknowledged is the existence of a self-sufficient economy in the countryside. The basis of this economy was agriculture.

Early in Chinese history one finds the saying that "the state was founded upon agriculture", which suggests that agriculture was the principal form of production in China during its thousands of years of feudal society. A specific analysis of China's peasant economy in this period will show, however, that it featured a close integration of farming and sideline production, i.e., handicrafts and animal husbandry. And alongside the peasant economy (consisting chiefly of farming) there were a number of independent handicraftsmen with a fair degree of expertise who were able to satisfy the people's needs for articles of bamboo, wood, iron and pottery. These varied elements of society came together at the temple fairs and market fairs and the bustling market towns. The market towns — centers for the rural economy — served the peasants as places to barter their produce and as supply points for seeds, farm tools and other means of production. Some of the larger market towns later became county seats with commercial establishments, places of entertainment, restaurants, taverns, teahouses and baths, where social contacts at various levels took place.

This gives us a picture of self-sufficient rural economies, each no more than a few dozen kilometers in circumference. Marx has said that the direct integration of agriculture and handicrafts, and the "simple production mechanism" based on self-sufficiency, "provides a key" to the secret of the long stagnation of Asian societies. This is precisely what held up the development of China's rural economy, an economy riddled with complex human relationships. The decisive factor in these relationships was the system of land ownership dominated by the landlords.

In the 1930s the Rural Revival Commission and other organizations of the Kuomintang government conducted an investigation in Shaanxi, Henan, Jiangsu, Zhejiang, Guangdong and Guangxi provinces. They found out the basic facts regarding land ownership by the different classes and strata in the rural society.

Table 1

RURAL LAND OWNERSHIP IN THE 1930S*

Class or strata	Percentage of households	Percentage of land owned
Landlords	3.5	45.8
Rich peasants	6.4	18.0
Middle peasants	19.8	17.8
Poor peasants and farm laborers	70.5	18.4

Ownership and cultivation, however, are quite different concepts. Although the landlords held much of the land, they did not cultivate it under concentrated management, but rented it out in small lots to landless and land-poor peasants. The peasants who actually worked the land had little land at their disposal and used only a few crude tools. A survey of Wuxi County

---

* Xue Muqiao, *The Rural Economy in Old China*, Agricultural Publishing House, 1980, p. 19.

shows a marked fragmentation of land management due to the prevalence of the above-mentioned tendency toward dispersal in farming.

Table 2

LAND MANAGEMENT IN WUXI COUNTY IN THE 1930S*

	Small-scale farming (under 10 mu)**	Medium-scale farming (10-20 mu)	Large-scale farming (over 20 mu)
1922	38.5%	36.09%	25.56%
1927	43.5%	35.7%	23.13%
1932	50.30%	34.13%	5.57%

This indicates that agriculture under the feudal system was mainly carried out in the form of a peasant economy based on the crude cultivation of tiny plots of land. The majority of those who worked the soil were poor and middle peasants.

Similar circumstances were revealed by rural investigations in southern Jiangsu Province, where the economy was relatively well-developed. An investigation made in 1949 at Hongqiao township in the Shanghai suburbs showed the tenancy relationships existed among 199 out of 312 households in the township.

Table 3 shows that landlords and rich peasants, accounting for 10.5 percent of the total number of households, owned 57.1 percent of the land, while the poor and middle peasants, who comprised 44.6 percent of the households, possessed only 21.3 percent of the land.

An intrinsic aspect of this rural social structure was ruthless economic exploitation, the main form of which was land rental. Besides this, however, the peasants were subjected to exploitation by usurious and commercial capital, which bore a heavy patina of feudalism and sometimes caused even greater harm to

* *Ibid.*, p. 24.
** One *mu* = 1/15 hectare.

Table 3   LAND OWNERSHIP IN HONGQIAO, SHANGHAI, 1949

Status	Number of households	Percentage of total	Private land (*mu*)	Percentage of private land	Rented land (*mu*)	Percentage of rented land
Landlords	8	4.0	483.0	38.4	3.2	0.9
Rich peasants	13	6.5	234.4	18.7	18.3	5.2
Middle peasants	32	16.0	155.3	12.4	100.4	28.6
Poor peasants	57	28.6	111.8	8.9	169.5	48.2
Merchants	49	24.6	182.3	14.5	26.6	7.6
Handicraftsmen and individual laborers	21	10.6	40.0	3.2	25.5	7.3
Peddlers	16	8.0	43.0	3.4	7.2	2.0
Teachers	2	1.0	5.5	0.4	0.8	0.2
Others	1	0.5	1.2	0.1	—	—

the peasants than land rental. Accompanying these forms of exploitation was stringent taxation. The peasants groaned under these combined burdens, barely managing to survive.

The well-defined social structure in the rural areas of old China had as its basis the antithesis between the landlord class and the peasants. Imperialist influences also entered the countryside after the imperialist powers invaded China, although the exploitation of the Chinese peasantry by foreign capital was pursued through the medium of the feudal relationships in China's rural society, which controlled trade and prices. Superficially, it would seem that comprador capital's domination of rural sources of raw materials would have temporarily provided the long-suffering peasantry with market guarantees; but this arrangement, which could be likened to drinking poison to quench one's thirst, generally worsened the peasants' plight.

Crushed by the forces of imperialism, China's national capitalists were very weak indeed. Those who turned to the rural areas often linked themselves with local feudal forces, a phenomenon determined by the fundamental social characteristics of the Chinese countryside before Liberation. The semi-feudal, semi-colonial nature of China's rural society dictated that the rural social structure should be characterized by ruthless domination on the part of the feudal forces. The *xiang** magistrates, who like the *baojia*** heads in towns and cities represented feudal oppression at the primary level, made life intolerable for the populace by their oppression and tyranny.

This situation made it inevitable that China's New Democratic Revolution would be directed against feudalism, imperialism and bureaucratic capitalism.

A new epoch in China's history began with the founding of the Chinese People's Republic in 1949.

---

* *Xiang* (township) was a former rural administrative unit under the county.

** The *baojia* system was an administrative system organized on the basis of households, each *jia* being made up of 10 households, and each *bao* of 10 *jia*. By means of this system, the Kuomintang regime enforced its fascist rule at the primary level after 1932.

Chinese history since then has seen a series of unprecedented changes which have been followed with concern by people the world over. These monumental changes, although beset with many difficulties and setbacks, were accompanied by an expansion of China's national economy and reforms in her social structure. In the more than 30 years between 1949 and 1982, the gross value of industrial and agricultural output in China increased 15 times at an average rate of 9.2 percent per annum, while between 1952 and 1981 national income rose 4.3 times at an average annual rate of 5.9 percent. Independent and relatively complete systems have been established in industry and the national economy, creating a stable base for the realistic and steady growth of China's socialist modernization. China's present industrial base is approximately equal to that of Japan in the late 1950s. China would have achieved a much higher rate of growth and a firmer industrial base had it not been for the "Leftist" mistakes committed beginning in the late 1950s, and the damage done by Lin Biao and the Gang of Four.

Within the enormous advances made in the national economy as a whole, progress in agriculture has been quite remarkable. The figures for 1982, as compared to those for 1949, show that in farming the gross output of grain was 706.8 billion *jin*,* having risen 2.1 times at an annual rate of 3.6 percent; cotton output reached 71.91 million *dan*,** rising nearly 7.1 times at an annual rate of 6.5 percent; production of oil-bearing crops rose 3.6 times and that of sugar more than 14 times. In animal husbandry, the number of large animals reached 101.13 million head, increasing by 68.5 percent at an annual rate of 1.6 percent; hogs, 300.78 million head, increasing 4.2 times at an annual rate of 5.2 percent; and sheep and goats, 181.79 million head, increasing 3.3 times at an annual rate of 4.5 percent.

Over the past 33 years, definite improvements have been registered in the land and equipment used in agricultural production. In the period from 1949 to 1982, a total of 86,900 res-

---

* One *jin* (catty) = 0.5 kilogram.
** One *dan* = 1 picul or 50 kilograms.

ervoirs were dug with an aggregate capacity of 418 million cubic meters, and the number of electrically operated wells increased to 2.62 million. The total area of irrigated land increased from more than 200 million *mu* in the early 1950s to 660 million *mu* in 1982. Improvements effected over 200 million *mu* of arable waterlogged land, 640,000 *mu* of saline-alkali soil and 340,000 *mu* of poor soil resulted in an increase of these areas' resistance to the effects of natural calamities.

Simultaneously, technical equipment for agricultural production has also registered marked increases. At the end of 1982, China had 812,000 large- and medium-sized tractors, 2.29 million walking tractors and 206,000 trucks for farm use. The total horsepower of agricultural machinery amounted to 230 million; electricity consumption in the countryside reached 39.7 billion kwh, and 68.12 million tons of chemical fertilizers were applied.

There was marked development in the field of forestry. Since the founding of the People's Republic, 420 million *mu* of land has been successfully afforested, resulting in a total forest area of 1,830 million *mu* in 1982. Of this, timber forests accounted for 1,470 million *mu*, shelter belts 120 million *mu*, economic forests 130 million *mu*, fuel forests 50 million *mu*, special purpose forests 10 million *mu* and bamboo forests 50 million *mu*. Timber reserves totaled 9.5 billion cubic meters, of which 3.5 million was exploitable.

In aquiculture, the gross output of aquatic products in 1982 was 5.16 million tons, an increase of 11.5 times over 1949.

Such large increases in agricultural production are closely linked with changes in production relations in the rural areas. These changes occurred in four phases: The first was from 1949 to 1952, when the basic tasks were to rehabilitate the war-torn national economy, complete the unfinished tasks of the Democratic Revolution and carry out land reform in the countryside. The second phase, from 1953 to 1965, was one of socialist transformation and the consolidation of the socialist economy. The main tasks in the countryside in this period were the collectivization of agriculture, the consolidation of the col-

lective economy and the development of agricultural production. During the third phase, comprising the ten years of domestic turmoil from 1966 to 1976, China's countryside suffered
enormous damage. The first two years of the fourth phase,
which began with the fall of the Gang of Four in 1976, were
marked by indecision until the Third Plenary Session of the
Party's 11th Central Committee held in 1978 drafted new policies for the rural economy which initiated a new economic and
social transformation of considerable magnitude and historical
importance. To give an accurate picture of this great transformation, we must trace its course back to the early years after the
victory of the War of Liberation and follow it step by step
through each stage of its development.

As we examine the past, we must not let our successes go to
our heads, but rather look closely at our shortcomings and focus
on various mistakes in policy and management committed over
the last decades. We should point out the roots of these mistakes and discover ways to effect further changes.

Regarding China's national economy as a whole, our work
in recent years has been generally directed toward economic
construction. This is what we refer to as the "strategic shift".
Henceforth, China's socialist construction will proceed in a
planned and systematic manner under circumstances of political stability and unity. Although changes in production relations
are necessary, they should not occur too frequently, and what is
more important, should never become divorced from the actual
state of the forces of production. Changes are not an end in
themselves, but a means of liberating the forces of production,
failing which they would lose all significance. This realization
has been gained through summing up positive and negative experiences gained over the course of 30 years of work, and upon
this basis we have determined a new orientation for China's
socialist construction. In his report on the work of the government delivered at the National People's Congress held in October 1981, Premier Zhao Ziyang pointed out that a new path
should be found for China's economy whereby better economic
results will be obtained with less investment, the economy will

develop steadily, and the people will derive real benefits. This important proposition in itself constitutes a new strategy for China's economic development. Under the guidance of this new strategy, the changes already initiated will be carried forward in industry, agriculture and all departments of the national economy until a fundamental reform has been brought about in the economic and administrative systems.

Highly significant among these basic changes are those that have taken place in agriculture since 1978, which are actually a continuation of the transformation of the socialist relations of production. The aim is to make production relations and management systems in the countryside conform to the present state of development of the productive forces in agriculture, and not to maximize collective management or effect the highest possible degree of public ownership. These sober and realistic guidelines are correctly based on objective laws rather than on concepts that go beyond the realm of actual possibility. Going beyond the limitations of pure ideology, these guidelines make the advancement — or lack of advancement — of the forces of production the sole criterion for the implementation of a policy. In fact, recent changes in systems of management transcend the limits of mere management methods and take on the nature of reforms in the system itself. At the same time, these changes make a creative contribution to the development of a model socialist rural economy. It will be remembered that the cooperative system in China's countryside underwent such a development in 1958 with the establishment of people's communes in which government administration was integrated with commune management; this later developed into the system defined as "three-level ownership by the commune, the production brigade and the production team, with the production team as the basic accounting unit". The plan at the time was for ownership to pass from the production team to the production brigade and then to the people's commune, thus transforming ownership from the small collective to the large collective, and then to the whole people, and ultimately from socialism to communism. In other words, it was to be a progression from a lower to a higher level. Classifications regarding this model were still based on the degree of public ownership of the means of production — the higher the degree, the more advanced the system. After more than 20 years of practice, it has become apparent that the fundamental thinking underlying this assumption is purely theoretical. Real life is much more dynamic. Today, production teams and brigades in many places have not — in the wake of increased production and economic development — ascended rung by rung up the ladder of public ownership. Instead, they have developed horizontally, setting up small-scale farm-produce processing industries and collective sideline industries, or in some cases construction and building materials enterprises or collectively run transport businesses, and even commercial and service enterprises. These teams and brigades have broken away from the limitations of concentrating on farming alone and of adopting the people's commune as the unit of production; they have entered the realm of market circulation, thereby, making up for deficiencies in the socialist planned economy and a lack of commercial channels in the socialist state. In this way, they have opened up new vistas for the development of the rural economy.

Over the past three decades, the Chinese countryside has proceeded along a path of development marked by zigzags and wave-like advances, a path exceedingly rich in content and profound in meaning. In this book, we shall take our readers on a retrospective tour of the course of this development.

Chapter II

THE MOST EXTENSIVE LAND
REFORM IN HISTORY

1. The Social Nature of the Land Reform

The revolution led by the Communist Party of China is, in essence, a proletarian socialist revolution. However, due to the particular characteristics of society in old China, the Chinese revolution had to go through the stage of the New Democratic Revolution before it could enter the phase of socialist revolution. The land reform carried out after nationwide liberation was not part of the socialist revolution, but rather a task of the bourgeois-type democratic revolution. It became the central task of the New Democratic Revolution for the simple reason that the principal aim of that revolution was to solve the peasant problem. The overwhelming majority of the population in old China were peasants, the most important sector of the economy was agriculture, and the sharpest struggles took place in the countryside. The feudal landlord class was the most brutal, corrupt and reactionary of the forces that disrupted social production, and oppressed and exploited the peasantry. The reactionary rule of foreign imperialism and China's domestic reactionaries had its social basis in the harsh rule of the reactionary landlord class over the broad masses of peasants. In this sense, the feudal landlord class became the tool of foreign imperialists and the Chinese comprador class. Thus land reform and freeing the peasantry of political oppression and economic exploitation by the landlord class was not simply an economic measure; it was the basic task of China's New Democratic Revolution.

Armed revolution versus armed counterrevolution was one of the major features of the Chinese revolution. Armed revolu-

tion refers, in essence, to armed uprisings of the peasant masses led by the working class, while armed counterrevolution
refers to a fascist military dictatorship implemented by the bu-
reaucratic-capitalist class with the support of foreign imperialism and reactionary Chinese landlords. Most deeply involved in
this struggle were the millions of Chinese peasants whose suffering exceeded that of any other section of Chinese society.

The victory of the people's revolution led by the Chinese
Communist Party marked the beginning of an entirely new historical era for the Chinese people. It was also a sign that the
Chinese peasant masses had thoroughly rid themselves of thousands of years of feudal oppression to become masters of their
own nation. Under such circumstances, it was only natural that
the peasants should urgently desire land; and for the sake of the
revolution, it was necessary to protect and support this desire.
Therein lay the strength of the Chinese revolution.

It is only natural to ask whether it would not have been possible, when the proletariat took over state power after the founding of the Chinese People's Republic, to transform the feudal
system of landlord ownership directly into socialist cooperatives,
rather than first going through the democratic revolution. The
answer is no. This would in fact have been impossible given
the situation of the Chinese economy at the time. Chief among
the many reasons is the fact that the social forces of production
had not yet reached a stage of development where cooperatives
could be set up. Nor were the peasants ideologically prepared
for it. The war was just over and the peasants badly needed
time to recuperate; the only way to satisfy the peasants' economic needs was to carry out land reform — to divide the land
seized by the landlords and rich peasants among the peasantry.
Any other course would have been detrimental to production
and, on the political plane, disadvantageous to the consolidation
of the worker-peasant alliance. The practice of the revolution
shows that the peasant masses enthusiastically rallied to the
Communist Party's revolutionary call during the New Democratic Revolution and gave their lives to this great historical struggle mainly because they were drawn by the Chinese Communist

Party's correct land program. In other words, the long-suffering peasantry did not join and support the revolution because of a conscious awareness of the great future communism held in store for humanity, but because they wanted to fight the landed gentry and divide up their land. The unsophisticated sentiments and economic demands of the peasants fitted in perfectly with the Party's political program during the New Democratic Revolution.

An examination of the inherent class nature of the peasants will be helpful to a deeper understanding of this matter. The peasantry and the industrial proletariat share one point in common: they are working people who suffer oppression and exploitation. This makes them natural allies and instills in the peasantry political confidence in the leadership of the proletariat.

After the Industrial Revolution, growing from their need to develop capitalism, the bourgeoisie also put forward slogans about reforming the land system. In practice, however, they rarely carried out thoroughgoing land reform, and in the end invariably adopted a policy of compromising with the feudal system. The land reforms carried out by the bourgeoisie generally took the form of issuing land bonds and giving the landlord class financial compensation. Just as in the past when slaveowners became feudal landowners, the landowners turned around and became owners of capital, while the peasantry continued to groan under the harsh exploitation of the new bourgeoisie. The only difference was that they were subjected to a different form of exploitation. Things, however, took a completely different turn under the leadership of the proletariat. The land reform led by the Chinese Communist Party not only satisfied peasants' economic needs, it also emancipated them politically — something unprecedented in the history of world land reforms. This is the fundamental difference between the land reform in China and that in the capitalist countries.

Another important factor specific to China was the political feebleness of the newly arisen bourgeoisie, a direct result of its economic weakness. Bourgeois political parties in China had raised the resounding slogan "land to the tillers", but they never acted upon it, nor was it possible for them to do so with any seriousness. In this respect they were even weaker than the bourgeoisie in other countries. For this reason, land reform in China could only be carried out under the leadership of the proletariat and its own political party.

Hence, land reform in China belonged by nature to the bourgeois-type democratic revolution led by the proletariat. It had, however, nothing in common with the reformist movements led by the bourgeoisie, since it was thoroughly revolutionary. And it provided the peasant masses with a profound and vivid education, one that strongly influenced them to eventually follow the proletariat onto the road of socialist revolution.

2. The Debate over Land Reform

Many differing opinions have been voiced at home and abroad about China's land reform. Among those who approved of the reform, not all understood it correctly. Some, for instance, maintained that it was an expression of the great sympathy felt by the Chinese proletariat for the peasantry. Such a view is hardly appropriate. As we know, the proletariat led the peasantry through the land reform for the sake of its own long-term objective of realizing mankind's greatest ideal — communism. Thus it was imperative to develop the social forces of production at the earliest possible time. Under the circumstances, only by smashing the feudal system of land ownership and solving the land problem was it possible to fully develop the agricultural forces of production; and only by fully developing the agricultural forces of production was it possible to create conditions for the development of the national economy. True enough, land reform inevitably promotes a higher standard of living among the peasantry and to a certain extent rids them of their poverty; but this does not mean that solving the question of poverty was a goal in itself. This problem must be solved, but its final solution lies in national industrialization and agricultural modernization, objectives which can only be realized by a thorough implementation of land reform. Herein lies the great significance of land reform.

China's land reform entailed parceling out land appropriated by the landlords among the landless and land-poor peasants. Some people feared that this would cause further fragmentation of land management and hamper the rehabilitation of the national economy. Such views had no foundation in reality. On the contrary, it was precisely under the system of landlord ownership that the land was sliced up into countless tiny plots and rented to the peasants. Although the land distributed to the peasants during the land reform was still managed with small production methods in regard to water conservancy installations, farmland construction and technical guidance, land management would gradually break out of the confines of small private ownership and, through various forms of mutual assistance and cooperation, eventually free itself of the limitations of the small-peasant economy.

Others believed that land reform was necessary for the country as a whole but not in those districts where feudal exploitation no longer existed owing to the development of a capitalist economy. From this arose the theory that there was "no feudalism in Jiangnan". Geographically, Jiangnan comprises Suzhou, Wuxi, Wujin, Zhenjiang and the suburbs of Shanghai. Imperialist invasions had resulted in the development of capitalism in China and in the coexistence of feudal capital, comprador capital and national capital. It cannot be denied that the development of a capitalist economy in the Jiangnan region brought about substantial changes in the local economic structure, though most of these changes occurred in the urban economies. Before the advent of capitalism, the feudal cities and towns — actually no more than extensions of the rural areas — were places where the feudal lords came to squander their wealth, and although handicraft industries had developed to a certain extent, they were very much limited by extra-economic exploitation in their management. The bourgeois cities were entirely different. As centers of industry, they had the advantages of concentration, in such areas as supplies of raw materials, transportation and marketing of products, and buying and selling of labor power. For this reason, they provided favorable conditions for industrial capital, which in turn gave impetus to commercial and financial capital, transforming the restructured cities into true paradises for capital. The rural areas under this influence also underwent economic restructuring in line with the needs of capital in the form of concentrating management, raising the percentage of marketable commodities and revising management methods.

However, the transition from a feudal to a capitalist economy in the rural areas of old China was extremely slow and lacking in direction, mainly because imperialism's economic invasion took place in the form of dumping goods rather than exporting capital, while the little capital that was exported supported processing enterprises set up to utilize cheap labor. In old Shanghai, for instance, about 60 percent of the cotton required by the city's textile industry was imported from the United States and India; and literally all of the wool required by its textile industry — comprising 80 percent of that in China — came from abroad. Similarly, the paper-making and cigarette industries could not have maintained production without importing raw materials. Imperialist capital's main interest in China was to appropriate labor and markets. The emergence of such a situation was closely linked with the grave backwardness of the feudal economy in the Chinese countryside, resulting in the backward feudal mode of production failing to undergo a thorough transformation by capitalism and suffering increasingly heavy blows from the outside.

Investigations of the rural economy illustrate this situation. In Wuxian County, a typical district in southern Jiangsu Province, the wealthiest landlord owned more than 10,000 mu of land. Landlords and rich peasants owned more than 75 percent of the land, and in one particular village as much as 90 percent. Some villages were populated entirely by landless farm laborers who spent their lives under the despotic rule of the landlord class.* The appearance of imperialist capital in the towns and cities of this region brought about no management reform in Wuxian's rural areas, and the same applied to all other counties. Statistics compiled by the local grain bureau show that if all the farmland in southern Jiangsu Province had been equally distributed, there would have been 2.177 *mu* per capita, while under the feudal land system, each landlord owned as much as 13.5 *mu* and a poor peasant no more than 0.3 *mu*.

Moreover, exploitation through land rental became even harsher in southern Jiangsu Province. This is best shown by the "contract rental system", the chief form of land rental in the southern Jiangsu countryside. When a landlord rented land to a peasant, he would stipulate in a contract the rent and the amount to be paid in advance, as well as the time, place and other details of payment. Since the landlords would collect the rent in the stipulated manner, irrespective of the harvests or the financial condition of his tenant, many peasant households went bankrupt. Another form of land rental in southern Jiangsu by which the landlords ruthlessly exploited the peasants was the so-called "right of eternal tenancy", according to which the peasant paid rent year after year for the permanent use of land which the landlord had acquired from the peasant by high-handed means. If a peasant were unable to pay rent for three years running, the landlord would take away the land, whereupon the tenant would be forced to leave his home village and face even greater hardships. The foregoing demonstrates the intensity of feudal exploitation in southern Jiangsu and shows that the insignificant development of capitalism had not brought about fundamental changes in the nature of society in these areas.

People who were not opposed to land reform when it was in progress wondered if methods of "peaceful negotiation" could have been used. The reply to this question is also no. Painful lessons in this respect have been learned in the history of China's land reform. During the War of Liberation, cases of "peaceful land reform" were recorded, but the landlord class fre-

---

* See *Liberation Daily*, March, 23, 1930.

quently managed to hoodwink the peasants. There were even cases in which landlords shifted most of their land to tenant farmers on the eve of land reform, retaining only a small amount for themselves. Due to insufficient mass mobilization, peasants who knew about this dared not tell the authorities. As a result, some tenants were labeled landlords, while the real landlords passed themselves off as poor peasants and even took over the leadership of the poor peasant associations. In such places it was often necessary to carry out a second land reform to rectify the errors of the "peaceful land reform". Such cases were, of course, quite rare. Another important reason why "peaceful land reform" was unfeasible was that feudal exploitation by the landlord class in old China was closely linked with harsh political oppression. If the peasants were to achieve complete emancipation, they had to rid themselves of both feudal exploitation and political oppression by landlords. Without struggle it would have been impossible to break down the influence of the landlord class, which could still dupe the peasants by such means as patriarchal clan relationships. Furthermore, in the case of landlords who were bitterly hated, popular indignation could not be slaked without struggle. Thus struggle was inevitable in carrying out land reform; for the peasants to liberate themselves it was indispensable to mobilize the masses and rouse the peasants to confront the landlords face to face.

3. Historical Development of the Land Reform

Large-scale land reform in the Chinese countryside took place only after the founding of the People's Republic. Before this, however, struggles to "strike out at the landed gentry and divide their land" were carried out in the revolutionary base areas by the peasant masses under the leadership of the Chinese Communist Party. These struggles provided a basis for land reform policy after the founding of the People's Republic.

The first land reform in contemporary Chinese history began in 1927 during the period of the Second Revolutionary War. At that time the upper bourgeoisie's betrayal of the revolution had led to the failure of the First Revolutionary War (1924-1927). Thereafter, the Chinese revolution shifted from the National United Front to the Worker-Peasant Alliance, which made land reform and armed revolutionary struggle its main work. In September 1927, the Party, based on a resolution made at the "August 7th Meeting", launched the Autumn Harvest Uprising — a peasant uprising centered in Hunan, Hubei, Jiangxi and Guangdong provinces. This uprising dealt a heavy blow to the forces of feudalism. Then in June and July 1928, the Party held its Sixth National Congress. One important point adopted at this congress was: "Confiscate the land of all landlords and distribute the land among the peasants." In October of the same year, some of the armed forces which had participated in the Hunan-Jiangxi uprising led by Mao Zedong entered the Jinggang Mountains and established the first revolutionary base. From then on, land reform in China spread rapidly.

A great turning point was reached in the Chinese revolution when the peasant and land problems became the revolution's main focus. The target of revolutionary struggle was now the countryside and the peasant problem was elevated to a strategic position. The struggles in the Jinggang Mountains took on historical significance, since they blazed a path for the victorious advance of the Chinese revolution. In the winter of 1928, based on a year's experience in land revolution, the Communist Party drew up its first land law; in April of the next year it drew up the Xingguo County Land Law; in autumn 1930 the Jiangxi Democratic Government passed the Provisional Land Law; and in 1931, the First Workers' and Peasants' Congress convening at Ruijin formally passed and promulgated the Land Law. This law, the reflection of five years of struggle since 1927, contained the following major points: First, it stipulated that the land belonging to all landlords, rich peasants, warlords, despotic gentry and monasteries would be confiscated and turned over to the peasants, thus boosting the peasants' morale and dealing a devastating blow to the authority of the landlord class and other reactionaries. Second, it stipulated that the peasants, after receiving land, had the right to dispose of it as they pleased; they could rent, lend, buy, sell, or bequeath it, give it to relatives or donate it to a public cause. This gave the peasants the satisfaction of real land ownership. Third, the law stipulated that land belonging to middle-strata peasants would remain untouched. At a time when the middle strata were wavering politically, this stipulation had the effect of reconciling and stabilizing this group of peasants, besides helping to unite the majority of the peasants. In 1933, the Central Workers' and Peasants' Democratic Government publicized two important documents — "How to Differentiate the Classes in the Rural Areas" and "Decision on Some Problems in Land Reform", both written by Mao Zedong. In these documents, correct experience — i.e., relying on the broad masses of poor peasants in launching thoroughgoing struggles against the landlord class — was upheld, and some erroneous ultra-"Left" actions, such as distributing no land to landlords and only poor land to rich peasants, were rectified. By this time, the land reform had reached its maturity.

On September 18, 1931, Japan launched a surprise attack that marked the beginning of its large-scale invasion of China. The national crisis assumed unprecedented gravity, and national contradictions became exacerbated. After the peaceful settlement of the Xi'an Incident and the formation of the Anti-Japanese National United Front, the Communist Party's rural policies underwent readjustment, the main thrust of which was to replace the policy of confiscating land belonging to the landlords and distributing it among the peasants to one of reducing rents and interest. This change was designed to unite all anti-Japanese social strata in China for joint resistance against the Japanese invasion. After the conclusion of the War of Resistance Against Japanese Aggression, the Kuomintang reactionaries resumed their anti-popular civil war and sabotaged the Anti-Japanese National United Front. Under these new historical circumstances, the peasants demanded a change in the land policy. In the course of the struggle to "punish traitors and settle accounts", some peasants had already escalated the struggle to the stage of wresting back their land from the traitors, landlords and evil gentry, which brought about a new situation in the class struggle in the countryside. Noting the enthusiasm displayed by the peasants in this struggle, the Party Central Committee issued in 1946 the famous May 4th Directive in support of the peasants' desire for land reform, thus opening the way for land reform by the masses.

In 1947, the Communist Party convened a national conference on land. This conference ratified the Outline Land Law of China, reaffirmed the guidelines of the May 4th Directive and rectified some unsatisfactory points in that directive; for example, the stipulations that landlords should be given more land and property than the peasants and that the land and property of the rich peasants should, in principle, be left untouched. The implementation of the Outline Land Law of China encouraged the poor peasants by mobilizing their political initiative and prompting them to join the army, support the war effort and take part in production, as well as in ensuring the victory of the War of Liberation. In February 1948, the Communist Party issued the "Directive on the Work of Land Reform and Party Consolidation in the Old and Semi-Old Liberated Areas" which made the following distinctions: In all old and semi-old Liberated Areas where the feudal system had been abolished, there should be no further division of land, although, if necessary certain inequalities in distribution should be readjusted so as to provide some land and other means of production to needy poor peasants and farm laborers; in addition, middle peasants should be allowed to have more land than poor peasants. In places where the feudal system still existed, land for distribution should be taken from surplus land belonging to the landlords and old-time rich peasants. In the newly liberated areas, no more adjustments should be made in the amount of land belonging to the middle peasants. These stipulations played an important role in ensuring the orderly implementation of land reform and in uniting all social strata, especially the middle peasants, in the rural areas for the common struggle against the enemy.

Summing up land reform of this period, Mao Zedong put forward two basic principles, namely:

First, the demands of the poor peasants and farm laborers must be satisfied; this is the most fundamental task in the land reform. Second, there must be firm unity with the middle peasants, and their interests must not be damaged. As long as we grasp these two basic principles, we can certainly carry out our tasks in the land reform successfully.*

The foregoing prepared the way in terms of strategy, politics and experience for the nationwide land reform which began in 1950.

4. General Line of the Land Reform

The founding of the People's Republic of China created the conditions for launching a nationwide movement for land reform. The Common Program adopted by the Chinese People's Political Consultative Conference, which then exercised the powers of the National People's Congress, stated that "Land reform is an indispensable condition for developing the forces of production and for the industrialization of China. Wherever the land reform is carried out, the rights of the peasants to own land must be protected. In those regions where land reform has not yet been carried out, we must mobilize the peasant masses, set up peasant associations and, through such steps as wiping out bandits and local despots, reducing rents and interest and distributing the land, put into effect the policy of the land to the tillers."

On January 30, 1950, the Central People's Government publicized the "Land Reform Law of the People's Republic of China", and Liu Shaoqi, on behalf of the Party Central Committee, delivered a report on land reform in which he set forth the line, principles, policies and steps for the land reform movement to be carried out in a planned, organized and methodical manner.

The general line adopted for the land reform was to rely on the poor peasants and farm laborers, neutralize the rich peas-

---

* Mao Zedong: "'The Present Situation and Our Tasks", *Selected Works*, Foreign Languages Press, Beijing, 1965, Vol. IV, p. 165.

ants, methodically abolish feudal exploitation and develop agricultural production. This line summarized the Communist Party's many years of experience in land reform and took into account the state of the classes and class struggle in the rural areas after the nationwide liberation. It embodied the following aspects:

1. Placing reliance, in the rural areas, on the poor peasants and farm laborers. In a systematic revolutionary struggle the question of whom to rely on is a matter of fundamental importance. The Communist Party's reliance on the poor peasants and farm laborers was based on two considerations: To begin with, from the point of view of class relations, the poor peasants and farm laborers were the proletariat and semi-proletariat of the rural areas. Although the Chinese countryside was feudal in its social makeup, the incursions of imperialism resulted in the appearance of a peculiar semi-feudal and semi-colonial social formation. The peasantry was no longer identical to that of an entirely feudal society, in that it no longer constituted an integral class. A process of polarization had produced a stratum of well-to-do middle peasants linked with the sluggish commodity economy. Few in numbers, this stratum nevertheless represented a new trend, and although contradictions existed between it and the feudal landlord class, such contradictions were considerably less intense than the contradictions which existed between the landlords and the poor peasants and farm laborers. "How to Differentiate the Classes in the Rural Areas" — a document that gave guidance to the land reform — provides the following explanations: "Workers (including farm laborers) as a rule own no land or farm implements, though some own a very small amount of land and a few farm implements. Workers make their living wholly or mainly by selling their labor power.... Among the poor peasants, some own part of their land and have a few odd farm implements, others own no land at all but only a few odd farm implements. As a rule, poor peasants have to rent the land they work on and are subjected to exploitation, having to pay land rent and interest on loans and to hire themselves out to some

extent." This state of affairs indicates that the poor peasants and farm laborers were, by their economic status, directly at odds with the feudal system, and that this antagonism was profoundly irreconcilable since it originated within the compass of feudal production relations. Secondly, it goes without saying that on the economic plane, the poor peasants and farm laborers desired land more urgently than any other class or stratum in the rural areas and, in political terms, were the most sorely oppressed and therefore the most militant.

2. Practicing a policy of uniting the middle peasants. Characteristically, the middle peasants were both laborers and small private owners. They did not exploit others, nor were they exploited themselves. This, of course, refers to the middle peasants as a whole; if examined household by household, some may have been exploited to some degree by the landlords, and some may have exploited others to a small extent. Generally speaking, however, they did not sell their labor; they owned a certain amount of land and farm tools, and were essentially an intermediate stratum. The middle peasants, who made up some 20 percent of the rural population and were good husbandmen, constituted an important force in the rural economy. They had to be securely united if land reform were to succeed. Mao Zedong said: "The positive or negative attitude of the middle peasants is one of the factors determining victory or defeat in the revolution."* The famous May 4th Directive also stated that it was necessary to "employ all means to draw the middle peasants into the movement and to make them benefit from it; on no account should the land of the middle peasants, including the well-to-do middle peasants, be encroached upon". The 1950 "Land Reform Law of the People's Republic of China" stipulates that "the land and property of the middle peasants, including the well-to-do middle peasants, should be protected against violation". Uniting the middle peasants was a consistent

---

* Mao Zedong: "Chinese Revolution and Chinese Communist Party", *Selected Works*, FLP, Beijing, 1965, Vol. II, pp. 323-324.

policy of the Communist Party during the land reform and in all aspects of rural work.

3.   Neutralizing the rich peasants. This was a major policy measure in the nationwide land reform movement launched after Liberation in 1949, a policy developed by the Communist Party in the light of changing circumstances. Such a change was necessary, timely and in conformity with the needs of the class struggle. Rich peasants made up four to five percent of China's agricultural population. Characteristically, the old-type rich peasants owned a large amount of land, good draft animals and tools; they engaged in labor themselves, but also rented out part of their land to other peasants or hired labor to help them cultivate their land; some also engaged in usury. Exploitation by the rich peasants was feudal in nature and in no way differed from that practiced by landlords. However, rich peasants differed from landlords in two respects: one, the form of exploitation practiced by them was less severe than that practiced by the landlords and, secondly, they themselves engaged in labor, which distinguished them from the landlords who lived off the labor of others. Of all the classes in the rural areas, the rich peasants were the closest to the well-to-do middle peasants and, in fact, easily confused with them, whereas they differed significantly from the landlords. Thus neutralizing the rich peasants not only reduced the scale of the target of attack in the rural areas and lessened resistance to land reform, but also obviated infringements upon the middle peasants, especially well-to-do middle peasants. Another fact was that the political attitude of the rich peasants had changed somewhat after Liberation. During the War of Liberation, because the balance of class forces was not yet clearly defined and since the forces of revolution and counterrevolution were locked in fierce struggles, the rich peasants took a passive attitude toward the revolution and moved closer to the landlords. After Liberation, the new political situation allowed the rich peasants to gradually move away from the landlords, making it possible to implement a policy of neutralization. It is evident now that the policy implemented after Liberation of neutralizing the rich peasants and

protecting their economy was entirely correct; it helped hasten the progress of the land reform.

4. Liquidating the feudal system of exploitation and liberating the productive forces in the rural areas. These were the fundamental aims and essence of the general line for the land reform. The feudal system of exploitation, which had existed in China for several thousand years, had brutally oppressed the peasants and hindered the development of the forces of production. The land reform eliminated once and for all the foundation of the feudal system — ownership of the land by the landlord class, which would have a far-reaching influence on the development of the social economy. However, abolishing the feudal system of exploitation and depriving the landlord class of its land and feudal privileges would inevitably arouse resistance on the part of that class. Thus in carrying out the land reform it was necessary to adopt stringent measures to suppress obstructive activities, sabotage and other unlawful actions by the landlords; otherwise, there would be no way to guarantee the success of the land reform. Thus with the exception of counter-revolutionary elements guilty of the most heinous crimes and local tyrants, individual landlords, so long as they offered no resistance, were dealt with under a policy of reform rather than physical liquidation. Law-abiding landlords were allocated the same amount of land as peasants and compelled to reform themselves through physical labor. Such a course of action helped break up the landlord class without adversely affecting the basic objective of abolishing the feudal system. This was the correct path to take since it promoted the smooth development of the land reform movement.

This fundamental thinking in the general line of the land reform constituted the basic class line of the land reform movement led by the Communist Party. It solved a series of problems, including those of whom to rely upon, whom to unite, whom to neutralize and whom to attack. As a strategic ideology for class struggle it attained a high degree of maturity, as evidenced by the practice and the great victory of the nationwide land reform movement.

5.   Measures and Methods of the Land Reform

Land reform was class struggle carried out in a systematic manner. To wage such a struggle and to carry it through to victory, it was necessary to fully mobilize the masses under the leadership of the Communist Party. In other words, land reform was a process of fully mobilizing the masses.

To mobilize the masses, land reform committees (organizations which directed the land reform movement) above the county level sent work teams to the countryside. The first thing these work teams did upon entering a village was to visit the poorest households and explain the Party's policies. The poorest peasants — those who had borne the brunt of class oppression — were often reluctant to divulge the truth; they held back to see if the work teams were really on their side. In such circumstances the work teams would go about their investigations patiently while explaining the aims and purposes of land reform to the peasantry. An important part of this lengthy process was identifying activists through whom the broad masses of poor peasants could be drawn into the movement. This part of the job was called *chuanlian,* or "linking up", and often succeeded quite quickly in mobilizing the peasants. In matters closely related to their own interests the peasants were highly sensitive politically and soon came to understand that the land reform work teams sent to their villages sincerely wanted to help them fight for emancipation. Thus, the peasants often called the work teams "our kinsmen sent by Chairman Mao" — a simple and straightforward manner of expressing their deep feelings toward the proletariat and its political party.

Once the policies had been explained and the masses mobilized, the process of class differentiation began, which lay the groundwork for electing the peasant associations, implementing the class policy and proceeding with the work of land reform.

Class differentiation called for serious and meticulous attention. In April 1950, the Administration Council of the Central People's Government publicized its decision on class differentiation in the rural areas and issued the revised versions of two documents drawn up in 1933 — "How to Differentiate Classes in the Rural Areas" and "Decision on a Number of Matters Related to the Land Reform". These were supplemented by "Some New Decisions Adopted by the Administration Council". These documents provided the theoretical foundation for class differentiation and land reform.

Class differentiation was based on the relationships involved in, and the degree of, exploitation. For example:

A person shall be classified a landlord who owns land, but does not engage in labor or only engages in supplementary labor, and who depends on exploitation for his means of livelihood. . . . A rich peasant generally owns land. . . . Generally speaking, they own better means of production and some floating capital and take part in labor themselves but are constantly dependent on exploitation for a part or the major part of their means of livelihood. Exploitation by rich peasants is chiefly in the form of exploiting the wage labor (hiring long-term laborers). . . . Many middle peasants own land. . . (and) own certain number of farm implements. The middle peasants depend wholly or mainly upon their own labor for their living. In general, they do not exploit others. Many of them are themselves exploited on a small scale by others in the form of land rent and loan interest. . . . Some of the middle peasants (the well-to-do middle peasants) practice a small degree of exploitation, but such exploitation is not a constant character and the income therefrom does not constitute their main means of livelihood. . . . In general, poor peasants have to rent land for cultivation, and are exploited by others in the form of land rent, loan interest or hired labor in a limited degree. . . . Workers (including farm laborers) generally have neither land nor farm implements. . . . They depend wholly or mainly upon the sale of their labor power for their living.

Class differentiation required mass participation. It could not have been done well, or even done at all, without the mobilization of and reliance on the masses.

Class differentiation was followed by the establishment of peasant associations and the unfolding of the struggle against the landlords. This struggle was carried out under the leadership of the peasant associations; work teams were required to assist the associations, but could not take over their function.

The struggles focused on the landlords who were most bitterly hated by the peasants. By relying on the power of the Kuomintang, these local despots rode roughshod over the people, preying upon them and committing all manner of evil. Many of their hands were stained with the blood of the peasants. Those landlords who owed blood debts and were guilty of the most heinous crimes were tried by provisional people's courts and given sentences ranging from imprisonment to death. This was necessary to assuage public indignation and to uphold justice. Their family members, however, and law-abiding landlords were dealt with according to their particular circumstances.

The stupendous spectacle of the movement is hard to describe in detail. One saw magnificently stirring scenes of politically awakened Chinese peasants plunging enthusiastically into the movement. The struggles were all the more dramatic and awesome in that the Party and government adopted a policy of arousing the masses to "liberate themselves". Assisted by the proletariat, the long-suffering Chinese peasantry rose up and, drawing from their own harrowing experiences, confronted the evil landlords and local despots with their crimes. They poured out their accounts of fathers murdered and wives abducted. Their sufferings — a mixture of economic exploitation, political oppression, ideological enthrallment and social humiliation — had reached staggering proportions and the hatred they engendered had accumulated through the centuries as fathers told sons and grandparents enjoined grandchildren never to forget the injustices practiced by the landlords. This eruption destroyed the old feudal order and paved the way to a new life.

Distribution of land was the high point of the movement. After burning the land deeds of the landlord class, the poor peasants and farm laborers received land certificates from the people's government. Once the peasants, led by the proletariat, emerged victorious from the struggle, they applied themselves to production and construction. The feudal land system had been buried once and for all.

A basic guideline upheld during the various stages of the land reform was to remind the masses constantly about the Party's policies. The Chinese peasantry had for centuries concealed their misery deep in their hearts. It was only when the proletariat stretched out a helping hand to support their struggle against the landlords that they found the courage to pour out their grievances. For this reason it was most important to instill in them the determination to struggle and confidence in victory. This was accomplished by educating them in such fundamental matters as the reasons for land reform, the justice of their taking back the land from the landlord class, the nature of the landlords' exploitation, and so on.

The nature of exploitation was a question frequently discussed during the land reform movement. Long the victims of deception on the part of the landlords, the unsophisticated peasants often failed to see the absurdity of such statements made by the landlord class that the landlords were doing the peasants a great favor by renting them land, and that without the landlords the peasants would have no land to farm and could not live; according to this logic, the landlords supported the peasants, for which the peasants should show their gratitude and submit to the landlords' dictates. The landlord class also propagated the ideology of "Heaven's will", claiming that the peasant possessed no land and had to rent it from the landlord because Heaven and the gods had ordained it to be so, and because the peasant's lot was to be poor while the landlord's was to be rich. To counter these reactionary misrepresentations, the peasants had to come to the understanding — acquired in the course of debates among themselves — that labor was the source of all material wealth and that labor creates the world. A number of questions were raised for them to discuss, such as:

Could land in its natural state become farmland without the labor of man? Could land produce grain and other crops without the hard work of the peasants? Was it not true that the idle landlord class was able to live in luxury and dissipation because of the "tributes" they exacted from the peasants? In the final analysis, hadn't the landlords acquired their fertile lands by exploiting the peasants? Through debates on "who supported whom" the peasant masses gradually saw the truth that labor creates the world. They understood that the relationship between the landlord and peasant classes was one between exploiter and the exploited, and came to see the simple yet basic truth that it was the peasants who supported the landlords and not vice versa. Once their class consciousness was raised, they threw themselves with full confidence into the struggle to settle their accounts with the landlords and local despots. The education the peasants received during this period was of paramount importance. It rectified the rights and wrongs long confounded by the landlord class, quickened the desire of the peasant millions to seek redress for all the injustices they had suffered, increased the impetus of the land reform and gave the struggle the motivation that ensured its success.

Land reform was a process whereby the peasantry waged a series of important political, economic and ideological struggles against the landlord class. It was also a profound lesson for the landlord class. The proletariat's policy was to liquidate the feudal system of exploitation but not the landlords as individuals. The policy toward members of the landlord class was to give them land and allow them to work under supervision so that they might reform themselves in the course of labor. All members of that class, with the exception of local despots and counterrevolutionaries guilty of the most heinous crimes, were given an opportunity to remold themselves. Those who cooperated could have their labels as landlord elements removed and become constituents of the laboring people. This thoroughly proletarian policy was necessary for the remolding of the landlords.

6. Some Policy Matters in the Land Reform

Many matters of policy had to be dealt with during the land reform. Their correct handling was important for the orderly progress of land reform and for the protection and development of the forces of production.

One important policy was concerned with protecting national industry and commerce. In a certain sense, this policy ran parallel to the land reform, in that the latter was a struggle against the feudal system while national industry and commerce fell within the category of capitalism. At the time, the Party's policy toward national industry and commerce was one of utilizing, restricting and remolding: utilizing their positive aspects for the benefit of the national economy and the people's livelihood; restricting the negative, backward aspects; and drawing national industrialists and businessmen into the Party's united front for the common struggle against feudalism. The situation in the rural areas, however, was extraordinarily complicated, since some landlords and rich peasants concurrently engaged in industry and commerce. This made it necessary to investigate their main source of income, and then deal with them in the light of the policy to protect industry and commerce. It would have been wrong to lump national industry and commerce together with the feudal landlords since they belonged to different historical categories and had different effects on the development of China's productive forces. Referring to this matter in *On the People's Democratic Dictatorship*, Mao Zedong wrote:

> To counter imperialist oppression and to raise her backward economy to a higher level, China must utilize all the factors of urban and rural capitalism that are beneficial and not harmful to the national economy and the people's livelihood; and we must unite with the national bourgeoisie in common struggle. Our present policy is to regulate capitalism, not to destroy it.

Of course, the fact that the Chinese revolution did not aim

at that time to destroy capitalism does not imply that capitalism is not a form of exploitation. It meant rather that exploitation by capitalist industrialists and businessmen was by nature different from that by the feudal landlord class, and that in the land reform movement the struggle should always be aimed at the landlord class, not at the national bourgeoisie.

During the land reform it was also necessary to draw a clear line between the landlords who lived by exploitation on the one hand, and, on the other, people in the rural areas who were short of labor power, had a little land and rented some of it out, or revolutionary soldiers, martyrs' dependants, workers, state employees, professionals, petty tradesmen and others who could not farm because of their professions and rented out a little land. The class status of these people was fixed according to their profession. No land was taken from them if the amount they owned per capita was less than 200 percent of the average amount owned per capita by the local people. Land in excess was requisitioned, although exceptions were made in cases where the land had been purchased with earnings from labor, or where the land belonged to those with no families or to disabled persons whose only means of support was the land they owned.

No discrimination was practiced against Buddhist monks and nuns, Taoists, priests or imams. They were given the same amount of land as the peasants if they were able to do physical labor, were willing to engage in agricultural production and had no other skills by which they could make a living.

7. Great Success of the Land Reform

The land reform movement in China was basically completed in the three years between 1950 and 1952. The area covered, including the old liberated areas, affected more than 90 percent of China's agricultural population. Land reform was carried out in practically all parts of China, except for such minority nationality regions as Xinjiang, Tibet, and Taiwan.

Some of the major accomplishments of the land reform are as follows:

(1)   The broad masses of peasants liberated themselves from the feudal system of land ownership. Between 60 and 70 percent of the rural population — mainly the poor peasants and farm laborers — derived real economic benefits from the land reform, and roughly 300 million peasants were distributed some 700 million *mu* of land. Before the land reform they paid the landlords as much as 600 billion *jin* of grain in rents every year. Now, except for small amounts used to pay agricultural taxes, all this grain went to the peasants themselves. This enormously increased their enthusiasm for production, and agriculture saw a period of rapid recovery and development. Gross national output of grain in 1952 was 45 percent higher than that of 1949, representing an average annual increase of about 15 percent, and was 16.9 percent higher than the largest output in any year before 1937. Large increases were also registered in such industrial crops as cotton, tobacco and silk. Cotton output in 1952 was 291 percent higher than that in 1949, and 52.3 percent greater than the previous record figure. Facts proved that land reform created excellent conditions for the emancipation of the agricultural forces of production.

(2)   Another result of the land reform was the expansion of the rural market. As the purchasing power of the peasants rose, sales of all types of daily necessities increased markedly. Statistics show that the gross volume of trade conducted in China in 1952 was 70 percent more than in 1951, giving strong impetus to the growth of industry. In the industrial sector, for instance, the output of many daily necessities was much greater than that in 1949, and equaled or surpassed the highest records in history. Taking the highest previous output of each product as 100, the output of cotton yarn in 1952 was 144, of cotton cloth 161, of flour 106, of cigarettes 145, and of matches 111. The growth of industrial and agricultural production also brought about a substantial increase in state finances. With agriculture as the basis of the national economy, increases in agricultural

production naturally resulted in the flourishing of other economic departments as well.

(3)   Political results. As the broad masses of peasants liquidated the feudal system of land ownership, they also toppled the local despots and lawless landlords and became the masters of their own destinies. A new situation appeared in the political life of the rural areas as the semi-feudal, semi-colonial economy and political system was replaced by an economy and political system of the people. This was a change of earthshaking proportions.

Chapter III

COLLECTIVIZATION OF AGRICULTURE

1. The Inevitability of Collectivization

The years between the founding of the Chinese People's Republic and the "three upsurges" in 1956 were a brief period of transition during which China could be described as a new-democratic society situated between a semi-feudal, semi-colonial society and a socialist society. The two basic tasks of this transitional period were: to complete the tasks left over from the New Democratic Revolution which could not be completed during the war years; and to initiate the transition to socialism. By 1953, land reform had been completed in all the rural areas except for a few minority nationality districts. At this time, the Party's policy for the rural areas was to call on the peasants to organize themselves, to launch a movement for mutual aid and cooperation, and to take the path of prosperity for all — while fully protecting the initiative of the peasants' individual economies.

The growth of the rural economy had become an irreversible trend after the land reform. During this growth, changes were bound to occur in the individual economies of the peasants. A 1953 survey in selected districts showed that only 30 to 40 percent of the peasant households showed little change after the land reform. Of the remainder, roughly 40 to 60 percent had expanding economies, while only 5 to 30 percent were in reduced circumstances.

However, the economic improvement in the life of the majority of the peasants was only one side of the picture; it stemmed from the fact that the peasants were now working on their own land and free labor had replaced slave labor. The other side was that the peasants still lacked substantial resources. Their tools and other means of production were both crude and insufficient in number. They could not withstand disasters, be they natural or man-made, and even in normal years were able to maintain a minimal existence only by practicing great caution. Most peasants had yet to free themselves from poverty.

The above situation is best illustrated by a survey made in 1954 of the changes in rural class relations after the land reform.

Table 4

RURAL CLASS STRUCTURE IN 1954

| | First six provinces* to set up cooperatives | | All other provinces | |
	Immediately after land reform	End of 1954	Immediately after land reform	End of 1954
Households in cooperatives	—	9.7	—	1.6
Poor peasants and farm laborers	54.3	23.8	58.5	31.4
Middle peasants	39.7	63.0	33.9	61.7
Rich peasants	3.9	1.8	3.4	2.3
Former landlords	1.9	1.7	2.9	3.0
Others	0.2	—	1.3	—
Total	100.0	100.0	100.0	100.0

The above table shows that in the provinces where cooperatives were first set up, the percentage of poor peasant and farm laborer households decreased from 54.3 to 23.8, and that of rich peasant households from 3.9 to 1.8, while that of middle peas-

* Hebei, Shandong, Liaoning, Jilin, Heilongjiang and Shanxi.

ants increased from 39.7 to 63.0. In all other provinces the percentage of poor peasant and farm laborer households decreased from 58.5 to 31.4, and that of rich peasant households from 3.4 to 2.3, while that of middle peasants increased from 33.9 to 61.7. Middle peasants were now the majority in the rural areas.

Another feature of the changing social structure in the rural areas was the difference in the rate of progress achieved by households within the middle-peasant stratum. Some rose faster than others, and a few actually declined, so that structural changes occurred within one and the same stratum. Most middle peasants, including both old and new members in this category, belonged to the lower brackets of middle-peasant stratum. These were the lower-middle peasants. A smaller number — the upper-middle peasants — made up the upper layer. A large disparity existed between these two groups in terms of ownership of land, draft animals and farm tools.

A survey of 201 households of the Hongguang Agricultural Cooperative in Taiyangping Township, Dingxian County, Hebei Province, shows the disparity among middle peasants in regard to land ownership per household.

Table 5

AVERAGE PEASANT LAND OWNERSHIP
IN TAIYANGPING, HEBEI*

Poor peasants	4.09 *mu*
New lower-middle peasants	4.30 *mu*
Old lower-middle peasants	5.40 *mu*
New upper-middle peasants	4.87 *mu*
Old upper-middle peasants	6.80 *mu*

A 1955 survey made at the Wujiamuqiao Agricultural Cooperative in Caozhuang Township, Jiaxing County, Zhejiang Province, reveals a similar disparity in the ownership of means of production:

* Quoted from the magazine, *Teaching and Research*, June 1956, p. 11.

Table 6

OWNERSHIP OF THE MEANS OF PRODUCTION IN CAOZHUANG, ZHEJIANG*

	Number of oxen	Number of large farm tools
New lower-middle peasants	0.14	1.6
Old lower-middle peasants	0.67	4.33
New upper-middle peasants	1	3.67
Old upper-middle peasants	0.80	6.6

Generally speaking, most agricultural households in various strata in the countryside had few resources at their disposal, as shown by a 1954 survey made in 20 typical townships in Shanxi Province. (See Table 7.)

The differences among lower-middle peasants are illustrated by the following types of households:

1. Big households with a large proportion of able-bodied workers, some with specialized skills. Although these households had few resources, they managed to get by, and their finances tended to improve. But they were hardly in a position to survive unforeseen calamities.

2. Small households with few able-bodied workers, although one or more had some specialized skills. They had many difficulties, but so long as nothing untoward happened to their chief bread-winners, they were able to make ends meet and better their financial circumstances to some degree.

3. Small families with few able-bodied workers and no specialized skills. These households continued to have financial difficulties.

4. Large households with few able-bodied workers and no specialized skills. Such households had great difficulty making ends meet.

---

* From the magazine, *New Construction*, Feb. 1956, p. 12.

Table 7

HOUSEHOLD RESOURCES IN 20 TOWNSHIPS IN SHANXI*

	Average amount of land per capita (*mu*)	Average number of draft animals per household	Average number of large farm implements per household
Overall average	6.62	0.56	0.84
Poor peasants and farm laborers	7.05	0.15	0.18
New lower-middle peasants	5.91	0.46	0.50
Old lower-middle peasants	6.15	0.49	0.78
New upper-middle peasants	7.41	0.8	0.98
Old upper-middle peasants	7.84	1.02	1.74

5. Households made up of old and ill people or widows and orphans. These had to rely on the assistance of relatives and friends, and faced the greatest difficulties among the middle peasants.

The five household types listed above describe the poor and lower-middle peasants. The greater majority of them were plagued by economic difficulties of one kind or another, and any unforeseen contingency, such as sickness, natural disasters or poor harvests, would at once plunge them into fresh misery. The most sensitive indicator of their circumstances was the practice of moneylending.

Moneylending increased somewhat in the rural areas after the land reform. This, on the whole, was a normal development permissible under government policy. Loans between individ-

* Quoted from *Developments in China's Agricultural Modernization* by Mo Yueda, Statistics Publishing House, 1958, p. 108.

uals and usury are entirely different matters. The reappearance of usury was a sign of class polarization. A 1952 survey made in seven villages in Xinxian County, Shanxi Province, showed that ten percent of the peasant households were compelled by natural or man-made adversities to borrow money at usurious rates. The loans, set for a period of three to six months, carried interest amounting to roughly 50 percent of the capital. The survey also indicated a resurgence of commercial speculation and exploitation by usury due to imbalances in economic development. Cases of buying and selling land were recorded, and a new stratum of rich peasants was beginning to appear.*

Another survey showed that as many as 31 households in Rongdang Village in Longmen County, Fujian Province, were in more instances forced to sell their land in order to repay their usurious loans.** The corollary to selling land was selling labor and exploiting farm laborers. The survey in Xinxian County shows that between 1949 and 1952, 8,253 peasant households sold a total of 39,912 *mu* of land, or 28 percent of the land they owned, causing a subsequent decline in their economic position. According to a survey of 19 villages in Jingle County, Shanxi Province, 880 of the 5,758 peasant households sold land, as a result of which 167 old middle-peasant households declined in status to poor peasants, similar to the way the status of 471 new middle-peasant households which had just acquired land declined during the land reform. These two categories, totaling 638 households, made up 72.5 percent of the total number of households that had sold land and 11.5 percent of the total number of farming households in the villages surveyed. Roughly six to ten percent of them were now classified as destitute households, their members now working for others as hired hands — the only exceptions being the few who had found jobs as workers in towns and cities or who rented land to cultivate.***

---

* Shi Jingtang, *Historical Data on the Agricultural Cooperative Movement in China,* Joint Publishing Co., 1958, p. 254.
** See *People's Daily,* Oct. 12, 1954.
*** Shi Jingtang, *op. cit.,* p. 252.

Such polarization in the rural areas was a natural outcome of the small commodity economy that had appeared after the land reform. Since it was not possible — or advisable — to hold up economic progress, and because exploitation could not be permitted to reappear, it was clear that the only way to deal with the matter was to organize the individual economies into agricultural cooperatives and seek common prosperity through collectivized agriculture.

A still more fundamental reason for the collectivization of agriculture, however, was the fact that China had embarked on the construction of a planned socialist economy in 1953. For large-scale development of the national economy, it was imperative that changes be effected in the small peasant economy to enable it to provide the large quantities of grain, cotton, oil-bearing crops, sugar crops and other industrial raw materials needed by developing industry. This was beyond the capabilities of the scattered and backward individual economies that had just come into existence. It was obvious that socialist industry could not carry on large-scale planned production on the basis of a scattered, unplanned small-peasant economy. This was one of the sharpest contradictions in the social economy at the time, the solution of which could only be found in the collectivization of agriculture.

2. What Made the Collectivization of Agriculture Possible?

Although the collectivization of agriculture was inevitable in the development of the rural economy, it was necessary to consider the feasibility of such collectivization when drawing up policies for it. Many factors were involved, the most important of which was whether or not the peasants, to whom land had just been distributed, would show any enthusiasm for such an undertaking.

Some economists maintained that caution should be exercised since the small peasants, being conservative by nature, held reservations about collectivization. This view was well taken. By reason of their economic conditions and mode of production, small peasants were indeed conservative. But a deeper examination shows that matters were not as simple as they appeared.

We know that small-peasant producers came into existence along with the disintegration of the primitive communes as a form of self-sufficient production. But never in the course of history did they establish their own independent mode of production. In all stages of human society they had always been relegated to a subordinate and dependent position. In slave societies, they served as a supplement to the slave-owners' economies; in feudal economies, they were the basis of the landlords' ownership system; in capitalist economies, they survived competition only by subordinating themselves to large-scale capitalist production. Admittedly, they are conservative, but it is precisely this quality that enabled them to adapt to all circumstances. Their subordination to others derives from the fact that they lack the ability to be independent. Hence when the socialist state economy assumed a dominant position in China's national economy, there was a good possibility that they would orientate themselves toward a socialist economy.

What, then, was the state of the national economy in 1954? As we know, it was one year before the start of the movement to set up agricultural cooperatives, which rose to a peak in 1955. The tasks set for the period of rehabilitation of the national economy had been completed in the main for industry and agriculture. A socialistic state economy was established and became the dominant force in the economy. This was a result of the special circumstances of China's economic development.

Before Liberation, modern industry accounted for only 10 percent of the gross output of China's economy, but it was extremely concentrated. National capital was very weak, while bureaucratic capital occupied the chief position in the national economy. It was the latter that served as the "entryway" for the socialist economy, as pointed out by Marx in his analysis of monopoly capital. In fact, after the victory of the Chinese revolution, this reactionary comprador capital, founded upon feudal and imperialist exploitation, became the most perfect material preparation for socialism.

After three years of economic rehabilitation, the socialist sector of the economy had grown in strength. Modern industry's share of the gross value of industrial and agricultural production rose swiftly from 17 percent in 1949 to 33 percent in 1954, and that of industries manufacturing the means of production increased from 28.8 percent of the entire value of industrial output to 42.8 percent over the same period. Thus the socialist state-owned economy attracted all other elements in the economy; it provided material conditions for the socialist transformation of capitalist industry and commerce and eased the way for bringing the peasants' individual economies into the orbit of the agricultural cooperatives. It also achieved rapid advances in domestic commerce, transport and communications, foreign trade and banking. That part of domestic commerce managed by the state and by cooperatives, for instance, accounted for about one half of the total volume of retail sales of social commodities and roughly 80 percent of the total volume of wholesale business. These material factors all drew the individual peasant economies toward socialism.

Human factors, however, were even more important in drawing up policies. As a consequence of the changes in the various strata in the rural areas after the land reform, the middle peasants now constituted the majority. But the term "middle peasant" is a complicated concept, and if the economically weak lower-middle peasants are set apart from the rest of the middle peasants, they can be seen to form a real majority in the complex fabric of the peasantry. This is shown in a survey of 42,306 households in Mancheng County, Hebei Province.

Table 8 shows that the lower-middle peasants and the poor peasants made up 81 percent — an absolute majority — of the peasant households in the rural areas. Beset as they were by a range of financial difficulties, the middle peasants were in constant danger of falling deeper into poverty; hence their enthusiasm for socialism. It was on the basis of this consideration that the class policy for the agricultural cooperative movement was

Table 8

CLASS BREAKDOWN IN MANCHENG, HEBEI*

Stratum	Number of households	Proportion in total number of households (%)
Poor peasants	8,432	19.9
New lower-middle peasants	12,258	29.0
Old lower-middle peasants	13,655	32.3
New upper-middle peasants	3,277	7.7
Old upper-middle peasants	3,073	7.3
Landlords and rich peasants	1,611	3.8

drawn up. The Central Committee of the Chinese Communist Party, in its "Resolution on the Agricultural Cooperatives" of July 1955, points out:

> It is necessary to formulate a strong force at the core of the cooperative movement. This force will be composed principally of active elements from two groups: poor peasants whose economic situation has shown no improvement, and lower-middle peasants from among the ranks of new middle peasants who were originally poor peasants; as well as active elements from among the lower-middle peasants who were formally old middle peasants.

The "Resolution" also stated that middle peasants were the long-time allies of the working class and the poor peasants, and that the latter must share their fates with them both in and out of the context of the cooperatives. Under no circumstances should the working class and poor peasants encroach on the interests of the middle peasants or expropriate their property.

Reliance on the poor and lower-middle peasants and solid unity with all middle peasants under the leadership of the Com-

---

* Tong Dalin's *The Basis for the Vigorous Development of Agricultural Cooperatives*, People's Publishing House, p. 13.

munist Party to build up an absolute majority in the rural population — this was the fundamental guarantee for overall victory in the movement to set up agricultural cooperatives.

3. How the Agricultural Cooperatives Were Set Up?

Setting up agricultural cooperatives began after the Party's Central Committee promulgated the General Line for the Period of Transition in 1953 and reached a climax after 1955. Earlier, movements for mutual aid and cooperation had been carried out in the old Liberated Areas, and China's first society for mutual aid through labor — according to extant documentation — was founded in 1931 in Caixi Village, Shanghang County, Fujian Province. Similar organizations were later set up in many places in the Red Areas. During the War of Resistance Against Japanese Aggression, a variety of organizations for mutual aid and cooperation in agricultural production, ranging from labor exchange groups and mutual aid teams to agricultural producers' cooperatives, were organized in the revolutionary base areas by the Chinese Communist Party. And during the War of Liberation, additional mutual aid teams and agricultural producers' cooperatives were set up after land reform was carried out by the Chinese Communist Party. The movement made further progress after the founding of the People's Republic when, at the end of 1951, the Party's Central Committee publicized its "Draft Resolution on Mutual Aid and Cooperation in Agricultural Production".

In those days, the movement for mutual aid and cooperation in agricultural production took two forms. One was the institution of mutual aid through labor, and the second was the establishment of jointly operated agricultural producers' cooperatives in which land was pooled in shares. Both forms were based on private ownership of the land, but the cooperatives were managed by all members and were thus a big improvement over the mutual aid teams where cooperation was limited to mutual assistance in the form of labor. These cooperatives were called semi-socialist agricultural producers' organizations or elementary agricultural producers' cooperatives. Later, the system of pooling land in shares was discarded and replaced by collective ownership of the land. This constituted a fundamental change in the land system, and those cooperatives which adopted the new system were called advanced agricultural producers' cooperatives. Developments and changes took place in the different forms of organizations for mutual aid and cooperation in agricultural production between 1950 and 1957.

Table 9 shows two small peaks between 1950 and 1957: the first in 1951, when 1,618 peasant households had joined cooperatives; and the second in 1955, when the figure reached 16.92 million. Immediately afterwards there came a big two-year upsurge, during which the number of peasant households in cooperatives reached 238.88 million, of which 226.87 million belonged to advanced cooperatives. This course of events, marked by twists and turns, gave rise at the time to significant debates among Chinese economists.

Some maintained that cooperative transformation of agriculture was not feasible in China's rural areas where the agricultural forces of production were extremely backward — consisting in the main of manual labor plus some animal-drawn plowing — and farm mechanization was totally absent. If badly handled, they insisted, efforts in this respect might only lead to some sort of agricultural socialism. Hence, it was advisable to put off the transformation for a reasonable period of time.

Others held that although no great developments had taken place in the agricultural forces of production, the rural economy had made rapid advances and it was not necessary to wait for the forces of production to expand in the countryside (as a result of the growth of capitalism) before carrying out socialist transformation.

Actually, Engels had already discussed this matter. He stated that the proletariat, after seizing state power, should organize the individual economies into cooperatives and not adopt a laissez-faire attitude toward them. Subsequently. Lenin successfully solved this question on the theoretical plane in the course of the Russian revolution. The fact is that the coopera-

Table 9   MUTUAL AID TEAMS AND COOPERATIVES, 1950-1957

	1950	1951	1952	1953	1954	1955	1956	1957
Number of mutual aid teams	2,724,000	4,675,000	8,026,000	7,450,000	9,931,000	7,147,000	850,000	
Number of households in mutual aid teams	11,313,000	21,000,000	45,364,000	45,637,000	68,476,000	60,389,000	1,042,000	
Number of elementary cooperatives	18	129	4,000	15,000	114,000	633,000	216,000	36,000
Number of households in elementary co-ops	187	1,588	57,000	273,000	2,285,000	16,881,000	10,407,000	1,602,000
Average number of households per co-op	10.4	12.3	15.7	18.1	20	26.7	48.2	44.5
Number of advanced cooperatives	1	1	10	15	200	500	540,000	753,000
Number of households in advanced co-ops	32	30	2,000	2,000	12,000	40,000	107,422,000	119,450,000
Average number of households per co-op	32	30	184	137.3	58.6	75.8	198.9	158.6

tive transformation of pre-mechanized agriculture, as with the "handicraft industries" in industry, is an inevitable transitional phase. Under normal circumstances, it is generally the developing forces of production that break down the old production relations: obsolete and backward production relations no longer suited to the developing forces of production must give way to new and progressive production relations that stimulate the forces of production. But at such times, social changes often play a decisive role. After the proletariat takes over state power, and when the socialistic state-managed economy holds a dominant position in the national economy and the social forces of production have developed to a certain extent, there arises the possibility of first transforming the relations of production in the rural areas and developing new ones so as to bring about further advances in the forces of production. The decision to adopt such a course was forced upon China by circumstances; it was not a matter of human volition. And given such circumstances, any attempt to withdraw would have been totally mistaken, if not impossible. Later, the method of first setting up cooperatives and then mechanizing became the fundamental line for China's agricultural development. This line now appears to have been entirely correct.

In 1953, the Central Committee of the Chinese Communist Party publicized two documents. The first was the "Resolution on Mutual Aid and Cooperation in Agricultural Production," which had appeared in draft form in 1951, and the other was the "Resolution on Developing Agricultural Producers' Cooperatives" drawn up in 1953. These documents were concrete applications in agriculture of the general line for the period of transition, i.e., the socialist transformation of agriculture, handicrafts and capitalist industry and commerce. They played an extremely important role in promoting the movement for mutual aid and cooperation in agriculture.

In July 1955, Mao Zedong's report on "Matters Related to the Setting Up of Agricultural Cooperatives" gave great impetus to the movement for the cooperative transformation of agriculture which lasted until 1957. The movement passed through

two main phases — that of the elementary agricultural producers' cooperatives and that of the advanced agricultural producers' cooperatives — or three main phases, if that of the original mutual aid teams is taken into account. These three phases
summed up the entire course of development of the movement
for mutual aid and cooperation in agricultural production. During this movement the cadres and masses learned many things,
and the social upheaval the movement engendered did much to
promote the political awakening of the Chinese peasantry.

4. Development of the Mutual Aid Teams

China's earliest mutual aid organizations in agricultural production came into existence in the 1930s in the wake of the
agrarian revolution. At the time, the revolutionary government in the Central Soviet Area — today the region around
Ruijin in Jiangxi Province — led to the establishment of mutual
aid associations for the purpose of redistributing labor power
in the rural areas. In some counties as many as several hundred thousand peasants, including women, joined these associations. Plow-oxen associations set up in the Soviet areas solved
the problems of households without oxen, which made up about
25 percent of the total. A survey showed that these associations,
in addition to regulating the use of the oxen, took care of them
and engaged in breeding. They also lessened the financial
burdens of their members, since the fees paid to rent oxen from
the associations were considerably lower than the cost of raising them.

During the War of Resistance Against Japanese Aggression,
agricultural mutual aid teams were quite widespread in the
Shaanxi-Gansu-Ningxia border region, and after the land reform, peasants in northern Shaanxi set up many types of mutual
aid organizations. Statistics compiled in 1943 show that there
were 4,588 "labor exchange teams" in the Guanzhong, Yanshu
and Longdong districts with 32,081 able-bodied workers participating, as well as 759 land-reclamation teams with 1,365

participants. The number of able-bodied workers in mutual aid organizations in the three districts mentioned above accounted for 36 percent of the total.* The economic situation in Yan'an proved that setting up mutual aid teams was beneficial to raising labor productivity. Figures quoted in the survey showed that peasants who had joined the labor exchange teams harvested 60 percent more grain than those who had not.**

As to how mutual aid and cooperation promoted increases in agricultural production, an article in the *Jiefang Ribao* (*Liberation Daily*) at the time summed up the following points:

1.   Labor efficiency was raised by having many people and animals working together.

2.   Time wasting was cut down by organizing all men and animals for effective labor, which in fact was tantamount to increasing the time spent on effective labor.

3.   Mutual aid heightened popular enthusiasm for production.   Able-bodied laborers worked with greater efficiency, while many "semi-able-bodied laborers" — women bound by household chores, school-age children, elderly people, etc. — pitched in voluntarily. Peasants previously known as idlers and loafers became good workers after joining mutual aid teams and were even cited as models.

After Liberation in 1949, the peasants were seriously lacking in farm tools and draft animals due to long years of exploitation and feudal oppression, and as a result the efforts of individual peasants to restore production were seriously hampered.   To help them in this respect, the Party and government set up mutual aid organizations under the slogans "Let the rich help the poor" and "Help the poor become rich". The peasants responded enthusiastically. Statistics compiled in October 1952 showed that there were 262,285 mutual aid teams of various types in Hubei Province, representing 30 percent of the peasant house-

---

* Shi Jingtang: *Historical Data on the Cooperative Movement in China*, Joint Publishing Co., 1958, Vol. II, p. 214.

** *Ibid.*, p. 223.

holds in the province.* Statistics of a survey conducted in Jiangxi Province in March 1953, counted 137,683 mutual aid teams comprising 1,326,000 able-bodied workers, or more than 18 percent of the total in the province.** A similar situation existed in all other provinces. For instance, the number of peasant households and able-bodied workers organized into mutual aid teams in Sichuan, Yunnan and Guizhou provinces accounted for 22 to 24 percent of the total peasant population.

On the whole, the mutual aid and cooperation organizations in the rural areas evolved by stages. There were two general types:

1.   Simple mutual aid teams of a temporary or seasonal nature. Characteristically small in scope, they were usually set up by a few peasant households for some special purpose, such as digging a pond, pumping water or transplanting rice seedlings, and were disbanded as soon as the job was finished. The participating households generally shared farm tools, cultivated adjoining fields, lived in proximity and trusted each other. The advantage of this form of mutual aid lay, first, in its similarity to the traditional custom of labor exchange prevalent among the peasantry. Developing out of the traditional practice, it suited the early stage of the movement for mutual aid and cooperation since it was easily accepted by the peasants. Secondly, it provided timely and effective solutions to problems in production through mutual exchanges of labor, draft animals and farm tools.

However, this form of mutual aid differed in several respects from the traditional practice of labor exchange. First, the mutual aid team was a regular organization with a leader. Secondly, members brought their own food to the households where the team was working, and when it became necessary to eat with that household, the rule was that economy should be practiced and the meals paid for. This was a great improvement over the

---

* *Collection of Reference Material on the Agricultural Producers' Cooperatives During the Period of National Economic Rehabilitation,* Science Publishing House, p. 983.
** *Ibid.,* p. 1055.

large sums expended during labor exchanges in the past. The poor peasants bore heavy burdens, such as the custom in Hunan Province of providing farm helpers with "wine at every meal and cigarettes 12 times a day", or, as in Jiangxi Province, with "two meat, two meatless and four side dishes at each meal". Third, the team kept unified accounts of labor provided, in keeping with the principle of mutual assistance and mutual benefit.

2. Permanent mutual aid teams, of which there were two types. The first grew out of the temporary team and might be termed a permanent form of it. Such teams were formed by the peasants on a voluntary basis after they had tasted the benefits of mutual aid and came to understand that they could solve difficulties by organizing themselves. This type differed from the temporary teams in several respects: first, they had a fixed membership; second, they generally had a permanent leader; third, they drew up a few necessary rules and regulations; fourth, accounts, instead of being settled after each job, were cleared at the end of the year or on major festivals, while some facilitated keeping accounts by instituting a system of work-points; and fifth, planning, although only of a very rudimentary type, directed the work.

In spite of the above-mentioned differences, however, the semi-permanent mutual aid teams were set by the peasants merely to solve the difficulties of the moment, and thus constituted a rather elementary form of cooperative.

The second type of permanent mutual aid team developed after mutual trust had increased between the participants, whereupon they began to look to mutual assistance as a means of developing production instead of simply solving difficulties. This was an important advance, for the new type of mutual aid team not only differed from the former type in terms of content; it actually represented a higher form of development. The differences between them were largely as follows:

(1) The work of this type of mutual aid team did not emphasize solving specific difficulties, such as repairing a house, building a pigsty or transplanting rice seedlings, but rather

on developing sideline production. Hence in some places they were called sideline production mutual aid teams. This shift in emphasis occurred because sideline production required certain skills, and after the mutual aid teams were set up the members helped each other in this respect, developed their abilities and instituted division of labor and management by categories.

(2) Once these mutual aid teams were set up, it became necessary to draw up plans for production and plan finances on this basis. This raised the teams to a higher stage of development.

(3) These teams did not limit their membership to friends and relatives or peasants with adjoining plots of land; instead they were mass organizations of a social nature formed on the basis of economic interests.

(4) They began to institute a public accumulation fund for use in production.

(5) Major advances were made by instituting a system of rules and regulations which covered assessment and registration of work done, bookkeeping, payment for the use of oxen and farm tools, and distribution of work. Such mutual aid teams served as a prototype for the organization of agricultural production and laid the foundation for the agricultural producers' cooperatives.

5. The Elementary Agricultural Producers' Cooperatives

China's first agricultural producers' cooperatives appeared during the period of national economic rehabilitation after the founding of the People's Republic, when mutual aid teams were being set up all over the country. It was then that the cooperative at Chuandi Village in Pingshun County, Shanxi Province, came into being.

Chuandi was a typical mountain village in the old liberated areas of North China. Situated in the Taihang Mountains, its poor land and limited water resources made farming difficult. Before the cooperative was set up there were ten mutual aid teams in the village, comprising 88 out of the 94 households. The villagers hoped that the mutual aid teams would enable them to expand production, but there were difficulties that the teams could not solve. First, increases in production could only be effected by deep-plowing the land, but there were too few draft animals and more had to be purchased. Secondly, more fertilizer needed to be applied, but there was no money to buy herds of sheep or goats (the local peasants' chief source of fertilizer). Thirdly, there was no way to use the excess labor resulting from mass participation in the mutual aid teams in a profitable and planned way. Fourthly, since the land was still broken up into small plots, it could not be used rationally or planted with the crops best suited to each location. Fifthly, the teams could not afford to buy large farm tools, not to mention tractors. The local peasants were considering organizing a cooperative, and when agricultural authorities decided in April of 1951 to set up agricultural producers' cooperatives on a trial basis, the inhabitants of Chuandi Village responded with enthusiasm.

As the cooperative at Chuandi Village was among the first elementary cooperatives to be formed in China, its success or failure had important bearing on the movement as a whole. One year later it proved to be an enormous success. In farming, increases were registered in both output per unit of land and gross output; labor productivity had been raised; and there was more farmland, due to the elimination of land boundaries and unplanted margins. Sideline production had expanded somewhat owing to a redistribution of labor power, greater investment and a shift to new lines of production. More important was the concentration of manpower, permitting division of labor by specialization and rational use of labor; concentration of the land, which made it possible to use the land rationally and to plant crops best suited to it; and concentrated management, which enabled the cooperative to use its funds rationally and purchase more means of production. The above also provided favorable conditions for large-scale future expansion.

The cooperative at Chuandi Village practiced the system of land shares. After deducting from gross earnings the investment for agricultural production, 40 percent of the remainder was used as payment for the land — as "dividends on land shares" belonging to the cooperative members — and 60 percent as remuneration for work performed, or "workpoints".

A good many elementary agricultural producers' cooperatives like that at Chuandi Village were set up experimentally throughout China. A point in common among them was the system of land shares and unified land management. Compared to the mutual aid teams, these cooperatives marked a major step forward on the road to socialism. In the mutual aid teams, all the means of production, including the land, were privately owned, and the individual peasants could do whatever they wished with them. In the agricultural producers' cooperatives, however, although the peasants retained in principle ownership rights over the land and other means of production (which entitled them to the "dividends on land shares"), they could no longer rent or sell these things. The same applied to the peasants themselves. When they operated as individuals, they themselves decided how to use their labor power, and this was the basis of the labor exchanges for the mutual aid teams. Once they joined a cooperative, however, all labor power was subject to unified management, which transformed the nature of labor. Meanwhile, since the products of the cooperative were the fruits of collective labor, it was impossible to determine who had created what part of it. Remuneration was handed out by the cooperative to its members in line with the principle "to each according to his work". These were indications that the elementary agricultural producers' cooperatives were different from the mutual aid teams, in spite of their recognition of the rights of their members to private ownership of the land and other means of production, and of their rights to withdraw from the cooperative at will. No longer private-ownership economic units, they were now semi-socialist in nature.

Furthermore, the socialist factor in these semi-socialist cooperatives gradually increased in importance as the economic basis of private ownership decreased in importance, along with advances in, and expansion of, production; increases in public accumulation funds, public welfare funds, public buildings and fixed assets; and with the changes in work organization, which was now based on unified planning. This qualitative transition took place gradually as the socialist industrial economy in the cities assumed a dominant position. Thus the cooperative economy became a component of the entire socialist economy instead of appearing as an isolated and incidental social phenomenon. Hence its enormous vitality and constant progress.

An important guiding principle in this development was the policy of mutual benefit. From the very outset, it was announced publicly that participation in the cooperatives was voluntary and that any member could withdraw from them of his or her own free will. Force or compulsion of any kind was absolutely forbidden. To ensure genuine implementation of the policy of mutual benefit, each cooperative worked out measures for investments in land, draft animals and farm implements according to local conditions, thus providing formal guarantees that the material interests of the peasants would not be encroached upon. All products of the elementary cooperatives were owned by the collective and constituted its gross income after deductions for expended means of production. Distribution was decided democratically at meetings attended by all cooperative members. After payment of state taxes, the cooperative withheld a certain amount of money for public accumulation and welfare; in this the cooperative's leadership had the understanding and active support of its membership.

When the first cooperatives were set up in the 1950s they received many-sided support and assistance from state financial, commercial, and credit and loan departments. They became models for the socialist transformation of the rural areas and served as examples and pace-setters for cooperatives set up at a later date.

Unified management made it possible for the socialist agricultural producers' cooperatives to accomplish tasks that were beyond the reach of the individual peasants and the mutual aid teams, such as farmland capital construction, unified disposition and rational use of manpower, and purchases of large farm implements and livestock. For this reason, their productive forces increased at a much higher rate. The output per unit of land achieved by the more than 600,000 cooperatives throughout the country which distributed income among their members in the autumn of 1955 was substantially higher than those of individual peasants.

Table 10

PRODUCTIVITY OF COOPERATIVE AND INDIVIDUAL PEASANTS, 1955*

(Unit: *jin* per *mu*)

Crops	Cooperatives	Individual peasants	Difference (%)
Rice	388.9	352.9	10.2
Wheat	120.4	112.1	7.4
Soybeans	130.8	109.9	19.0
Cotton	41.8	33.2	25.9
Cured tobacco	169.9	157.0	8.2
Sugarcane	5,943.0	5,425.7	9.5
Beetroot	1,797.4	1,719.7	4.5
Peanuts	207.3	177.8	16.6
Rapeseed	71.7	65.0	10.3

These figures show the incontestable superiority of the cooperatives over the individual peasants as economic units. In the meantime, the polarization that had begun to take place in the rural areas before the cooperatives came into being by and large came to a halt.

Peasants are realists. When individual peasants saw for themselves the superiority of the agricultural producers' cooperatives, they were eager to join or set up such collectives. This is a major reason for the rapid progress of agricultural collectivization in China.

* Mo Yueda: *Development of the Agricultural Cooperative Movement in China,* Statistical Publishing House, 1958, p. 96.

6. The "Hightide" and the Advanced Agricultural Producers' Cooperatives

A common feature of the agricultural cooperative movements that took place in various parts of China in 1953 was that they began rather slowly and gradually picked up speed. In 1953, there were 15,000 cooperatives in China, comprising 273,000 households. The following year, there were 114,000 cooperatives with 2,300,000 households. In 1955, the number of cooperatives jumped to 634,000; a total of 16,921,000 peasant households had now joined cooperatives. In 1956, there were 756,000 cooperatives, comprising 117.82 million households. The following year, there were 789,000 cooperatives with 121.05 million households.

The cause behind such a pattern of development lay in the peasants' gradual understanding of the cooperatives. They had to see for themselves that the cooperatives reaped better harvests than individual peasants before volunteering to join up. Without such willingness on their part the cooperatives could not have been consolidated. A case in point is Xicun township in Kunshan County, Jiangsu Province, as described in "This Township Went Cooperative in Two Years" in *The Hightide of Socialism in China's Rural Areas*. Two cooperatives set up in this township in the winter of 1953 were a success: production developed and the incomes of its members increased. Ten more cooperatives set up in the autumn of the following year also did well, and by autumn 1955 the whole township had gone cooperative, with 89 percent of the peasant households belonging to cooperatives. Those who did not join — former landlord and rich peasant households — were also taken in at a later date.

The experience of this township shows that the cooperative movement developed by and large according to a pattern: When the first batch of cooperatives was set up, the peasants would wait and watch for a while; then additional cooperatives would be organized, and the peasants would again wait to see how they turned out. Progress was not always smooth, but on the whole the movement increased in terms of both size and tempo. In Sichuan Province, the movement was said to be "advancing by leaps". As in the foregoing example, the key factor was how well the first models turned out. If they were successful, there would be fewer problems later on. Generally speaking, if ten percent of the households joined the first batch of cooperatives, as many as 50 percent might join the second batch.

And so it was that the movement for the cooperativization of agriculture, after three years of steady progress, began to leap forward in the second half of 1955, culminating in the famous "hightide". By the end of the same year, in many provinces and municipalities practically all the peasant households had joined cooperatives, and in many others the majority had joined. In Liaoning and Beijing, 90 percent of the peasant households had entered cooperatives; in Shanxi, Tianjin, Anhui, Hebei, Shanghai and Heilongjiang, 80 to 90 percent had joined; in Henan, Hubei, Jilin and Gansu, 70 to 79 percent; in Shandong, Inner Mongolia, Zhejiang, Jiangxi and Fujian, 60 to 69 percent; and in Jiangsu, Qinghai and Sichuan, 50 to 59 percent. By 1956, cooperativization had been completed throughout the country, and collectively owned economic units became the chief sector in the rural economy. The Chinese countryside entered the socialist era, thus marking another major transformation following the land reform.

Beginning in 1956, the cooperativization of agriculture, which was now sweeping the whole country, shifted its focus to the setting up of advanced agricultural producers' cooperatives.

The major difference between the elementary and advanced cooperatives was that private ownership of the land was retained in the former, but not in the latter. Thus, in the elementary cooperatives, each peasant household had to be consulted and their approval obtained when farmland capital construction or plans for the use of the land were contemplated. Member households naturally considered their own economic interests first when such matters were brought up, frequently resulting in nothing being accomplished because one individual would disagree. A village in Neiqiu County, Hebei Province, planned to build a dyke which would protect 100 *mu* of good farmland from flooding, but the project had to be dropped since the owner of the land on which the dyke was to be built would not agree. Many difficulties also arose from the fact that draft animals and farm tools were privately owned in the elementary cooperatives. After bringing a horse into the cooperative, for instance, the horse's owner always feared that it would be overworked, and other members, to avoid trouble, would not use the animal to its full capacity. Moreover, the payment of dividends on land, draft animals and farm tools invested in the cooperatives placed limits on the amount of funds available for expansion of production.

In these circumstances, most member households began to demand that the elementary cooperatives be turned into cooperatives of the advanced type. Such "escalation" took place on a massive scale in the rural areas during the second half of 1955 and the first half of 1956. Socialist education among the peasants was reinforced to put this "escalation" on a suitable footing; facts were cited to show the peasants that upgrading the cooperatives would not be disadvantageous to them, even to those who owned comparatively more land, draft animals and farm implements. Actually, since the cooperative movement took place not long after the land reform and before polarization in the rural areas had reached serious proportions, few difficulties were encountered in the course of escalation. And no sooner had the process been completed than the advantages of the advanced cooperatives began to manifest themselves:

1. Public ownership of the land made it possible for the cooperatives to plan the use of the land and carry out necessary farmland capital construction;

2. Public ownership of the means of production enabled the cooperatives to make concentrated use of large farm tools and draft animals through division of labor, and to improve farming techniques, reform the cultivation system and develop sideline production.

3. Relieved of the need to pay dividends, the cooperatives could devote more funds to accumulation and expanding production.

4. Planned management and production management became easier. Each cooperative was subdivided into several production teams which planted crops that suited the land, and guaranteed to supply a certain amount of produce and profits to the cooperative. The cooperative in turn rewarded the teams for whatever they produced over and above their quotas.

With these advantages, the advanced cooperatives made better use of the agricultural forces of production and effected large increases in output value. And of the various classes and strata in the countryside, those who derived the greatest benefit were the poor peasants and lower-middle peasants, who made up the overwhelming majority of the rural population.

Table 11, based on a 1956 investigation of 564 cooperatives in 20 provinces and regions, shows the increase and decrease in income among households of various classes or strata in the rural areas.

The hightide of the cooperative movement in the Chinese countryside coincided with similar movements for the socialist transformation of capitalist industry and commerce in the cities and handicraft industries in urban and rural areas. In fact, the socialist transformation of agriculture provided to a large extent the motive force and the proper conditions for the other two transformations. The completion of the cooperative movement in agriculture, for instance, severed the economic ties between capitalist industry and commerce and the individual peasants, especially the rich peasants. This deprived the former of their sources of materials and compelled them to accept socialist transformation. This was one of the most successful tactics used in China for the peaceful transformation of the capitalist sector of the economy and for effecting the socialist revolution.

The combination of the three above-mentioned transformations brought about an enormous advance in the socialist sector of the economy. And by 1956, a massive economic revolution

Table 11

INCREASE AND DECREASE OF RURAL HOUSEHOLD INCOME, 1956*

	Total number of households	Those with increased incomes (%)	Those with incomes unchanged (%)	Those with reduced incomes (%)
Poor peasants	65,394	69.34	4 13	26.53
New lower-middle peasants	39,184	72.89	4.10	23.01
Old lower-middle peasants	35,333	64.26	4.61	31.13
New upper-middle peasants	17,268	67.45	4.53	28.02
Old upper-middle peasants	23,542	61.92	4.88	33.20
Other laboring people	2,768	62.50	6.43	31.07
Rich peasants	5,194	57.78	3.81	38.41
Landlords and other exploiters	6,671	65.48	4.55	29.97
Total	195,354	67.53	4.38	28.09

* Su Xing: *Socialist Transformation of China's Agriculture*, People's Publishing House, p. 151.

had achieved its historic mission: China, a country with nearly one-fourth of the world's population, completed the transition from a New Democratic society to a socialist society.

7. Changes in the Rural Economy After the Cooperative Movement

Marked changes took place in the rural economy after the cooperative movement.

Foremost among these was a large growth in the agricultural forces of production. An investigation of 101 agricultural producers' cooperatives conducted in Shanxi Province showed that the local peasants' total income from farm and sideline production rose from 6.69 million yuan in 1955 (before the setting up of the cooperatives) to 7.88 million yuan in 1957, an increase of 17.81 percent. Such a rate of increase was unprecedented either before or after Liberation. The incomes of the villagers where the 101 cooperatives were established increased by a total of only 32.4 percent in the 13 years from 1937 to 1949, and by 26.79 percent in the six years from 1949 to 1955.*

A breakdown of incomes from sources other than farming explains the rapid rate of increase in total income after the cooperative movement. (See Table 12.)

The rapid development of a diversified economy after the cooperatives came into existence was made possible by the fact that they had a great deal more funds and manpower at their disposal.

Other benefits of the cooperative movement may be summed up as follows:

1. The elimination of boundaries between individual family plots made it possible to use the land more rationally, since large plots were farmed under unified plans and double-cropping increased.

---

* *Survey of the Rural Economy in Shanxi.* Shanxi People's Publishing House, 1959. Vol. I, p. 1.

Table 12

NON-FARMING INCOME, 1936-1957
(Selected Years)

(Unit: yuan)

	Forestry products	Animal husbandry	Sidelines
1936	100	100	100
1949	87.16	78.86	89.00
1952	98.04	111.55	103.64
1955	185.90	152.76	123.72
1956	208.05	173.88	145.98
1957	452.08	197.37	156.08

2.   The concentration of manpower facilitated division of labor. Some manpower could be freed from the current year's production tasks and engage in long-term construction, thus creating conditions for carrying out large-scale capital construction.

3.   Rural industries and sidelines could be developed to make better use of local natural resources.

4.   Rational use of both stronger and weaker workers in the collective economy brought into play the creative energies of many more people, especially women.

The effects of cooperativization on agricultural production are illustrated by the following comparisons of national agricultural output and output value in 1952 and 1957:

1.   Grain: Gross national production of grain, 327.83 billion *jin* in 1952, was 390.09 billion *jin* in 1957, an increase of 62.26 billion *jin*, or nearly 20 percent, representing an average annual increase of more than 3.8 percent.

2.   Cash crops: Output of cotton, 26.07 million *dan* in 1952, rose to 32.8 million *dan* in 1957, an increase of 6.73 million *dan*; sugarcane production, 142.32 million *dan* in 1952, reached 207.85 million *dan* in 1957, an increase of 63.53 million *dan*;

and beetroot, 9.57 million *dan* in 1952, rose to 30.02 million *dan* in 1957, registering an increase of 20.45 million *dan*.

3. Animal husbandry: The number of hogs increased from 89.77 million at the end of 1952 to 145.9 million in 1957; and of sheep and goats from 61.78 million at the end of 1952 to 98.58 million in 1957.

4. Aquatic products: Gross production rose from 1.67 million tons in 1952 to 3.12 million tons in 1957.

5. Gross value of agricultural production, calculated according to 1952 fixed prices, rose from 48.4 billion yuan in 1952 to 60.4 billion yuan in 1957, an increase of 12 billion yuan.

Beginning in 1957, a series of changes took place in the agricultural economy: the percentage of marketable produce increased with a corresponding rise in the amount of commodities supplied to the countryside by industrial departments; and growing economic ties between town and countryside resulted in an increase in currency circulation between the two. In keeping with this, the proportion of national income from agriculture increased substantially, as shown by the figures for 1952 and 1957.

Table 13

NATIONAL AGRICULTURAL INCOME
IN 1952 AND 1957

	1952	1957
National income from agriculture* (million yuan)	34,000	42,500
Proportion in gross national income (%)	57.7	46.8

Although there was a fairly large increase in the agricultural population in this period, the amount of national income created on the average by each person in the rural areas rose from 69 yuan in 1952 to 79 yuan in 1957, or from 196 yuan per able-

* Calculated according to fixed prices for the same year.

bodied worker in 1952 to 247 yuan in 1957.

From the economic point of view, the most important of these changes was the increase in the percentage of marketable produce, a major indication of the transformation of the rural economy. Such an increase meant that cooperatives and other sectors of the peasantry could be integrated through exchanges, that the economies of city and countryside could establish closer links, and that urban industry, transportation and communication, commercial departments, and industrial and mining districts would obtain more farm produce, which in turn would promote further advances in the national economy. It also enabled the rural economy to free itself from the limitations of a natural economy and make the transition to a commodity economy. This, in essence, meant increased socialization of rural labor. The peasants no longer worked simply to keep themselves clothed and fed; they were now working for society. Such a change could hardly have been effected in an economy of peasants working as individuals.

A few figures will illustrate the increase of the marketable ratio of agricultural produce. The following figures are drawn from statistics on the state purchases of agricultural produce before and after the organization of agricultural cooperatives:

Table 14

STATE PURCHASES OF AGRICULTURAL PRODUCE, 1950-1957

	1950	1952	1957
Gross purchase of agricultural produce (million yuan)	—	9,010	17,650
Cotton (thousand *dan*)	—	20,001	27,662
Hogs (thousands)	815	5,072	36,951
Sheep and goats (thousands)	33	1,660	5,128

These initial changes augured well for the development of China's rural economy.

8. Birth and Growth of the People's Commune System

The agricultural producers' cooperatives set up in the Chinese countryside were a form of socialist economic organization where ownership was by the collective. They represented a momentous transformation in the Chinese countryside: the demise of the system of private land ownership and the establishment of socialist relations of production. Ordinarily, general laws of development would have dictated a period of relative stability and consolidation after such a great transformation, but developments on the political and economic scene in 1958 deviated from any such laws, culminating in the birth of a new form of organization — the people's commune. The people's commune was the product of an outburst of enthusiasm, and the complications it experienced provide important historical lessons for Chinese agriculture.

At the outset of the people's commune movement, the slogan "Great Leap Forward" was raised. This in essence was an expression of the people's yearning for a better life. But all slogans, regardless of the intentions they represent, remain mere wishful thinking if they run counter to objective laws of development. Later experience showed that the Great Leap Forward was actually rash and premature. Together with its coeval, the people's commune, it was destined to be the center of acute struggles. The antitheses in this struggle were the "wind of exaggeration" and the "communist wind", both of which arose in the course of the Great Leap Forward.

The "wind of exaggeration" was the practice of claiming the existence of nonexistant achievements. The inflated claims with regard to per-hectare yields, for instance, reached extraordinary proportions and were completely at variance with the laws of nature.

The "communist wind" referred to impracticable and unscientific attempts, contrary to all laws of social development, to set up a "communist society" by means of equal distribution, before the forces of production and material goods production had reached the state of development necessary for such a transition. The "communist wind" was the product of petty bourgeois ideology and had nothing in common with Marxist communism. The presence in China of such nonscientific and petty bourgeois ideological trends is due to the preponderance in the Chinese population of small producers whose world view contained elements of utopianism. Actually, these ideological trends can be traced far back in Chinese history. For centuries the idea that "inequality is more to be feared than poverty" has endured among these small producers. This mentality provided the background to the "communist wind".

But the "communist wind" which appeared during the 1958 Great Leap Forward differed from the egalitarian thinking of the past in that it was served up under the name of scientific Marxism. Gaining ascendancy for a period of time, it obstructed socialist construction in the Chinese countryside. Fortunately, the Party and government soon discovered this state of affairs and adopted corrective measures. As a result, the people's communes, which had been troubled by the "communist wind" from birth, took the road of healthy development.

The course of events will be better understood if we review the situation in the countryside after the setting up of the agricultural cooperatives.

The setting up of agricultural cooperatives was completed in the main in 1956. After collectivization, the peasants decided to further increase production by carrying out large-scale capital construction in water conservancy, and in some places there were movements to combine individual cooperatives into larger ones called "communist communes". The Party and government, however, used the term "people's communes" when referring to them in official documents. But the word "communist" persisted in the countryside in the popular saying "Communism is paradise and the people's commune is the bridge (leading to it)". Moreover, such incorrect practices as providing everyone with free food and indulging everyone in a comprehensive supply system persisted. At the end of 1958, the Eighth Session of the Party's Sixth Central Committee passed the "Resolution on Some Matters Pertaining to the People's Communes" in which lines of demarcation were put forward to counter the tendency toward rash and overhasty advances. The "Resolution" defined the economic conditions necessary for a transition from collective ownership to ownership by the whole people and from socialism to communism, and criticized such erroneous slogans as "Institute ownership by the whole people at once" and "Enter communist society at the double". These measures had some effect in curbing the "communist wind" in the countryside.

But the "Left" tendency had not been thoroughly rectified, and in some places continued to manifest itself in a most serious manner. To remedy this state of affairs, the Party convened a meeting at Lushan in September 1959. Unfortunately, the meeting did not achieve its purpose. Instead, a movement to oppose Right tendencies was launched, which had the effect of aggravating the "Left" mistakes in the agricultural economy and causing grave setbacks in the Party's work in the rural areas. It was only after the Party's Central Committee issued a letter in November 1960, containing directives on policy matters related to the people's communes, that systematic efforts were made to find solutions for major policy matters. Firm measures were taken to rectify egalitarianism and indiscriminate transfer of resources among rural production units. Three-level ownership (by the commune, the production brigade and the production team), with the production team as the basic unit, became the basic system of administration for the people's communes. The "Rules and Regulations for the Work of the People's Communes" (promulgated in January 1961), also known as the "Sixty Articles", formally made the production team the basic accounting unit, thus paving the way for smoother advances by the people's commune.

The "three-level system of ownership with the production team as the basic unit" was a system of administration worked out in the course of practice. Its main feature was the division of the commune into three levels of administration. The commune members' productive activities and distribution of income was organized by the production team, which was thus called the basic accounting unit. The people's commune and production brigades were administrative units, but they also ran some collective undertakings which retained part of their income as accumulation funds, while the rest of it went back to the production teams in one form or another. The wages of commune members working in enterprises run by the commune or production brigades were paid to the workers' production teams, and these commune members shared in the production teams' distribution of income like everyone else. This system of administration was highly flexible, but it had the disadvantage of imposing too many restrictions — particularly since the people's commune combined government administration with economic management — and there were frequent infringements of the teams' rights to manage their own productive activities. More than two decades have elapsed since the promulgation of the "Rules and Regulations on the Work of the People's Communes" in 1960. Along with the growth of the rural economy and the readjustment and reforms in the national economy, the people's commune system will certainly see constant improvement as it continues to sum up its experience.

Whatever future improvements are made in the people's commune system, there are at least four features of its administrative system worth noting:

1.　Unified management of agricultural machinery and equipment. According to 1982 statistics, rural people's communes throughout China had farm machinery totaling 220 million horsepower, of which large and medium-sized tractors accounted for 35.53 million horsepower; walking tractors, 27 million horsepower; farm trucks, 8.3 million horsepower; irrigation and drainage equipment, 71.2 million horsepower; and other agricultural machinery, 54.2 million horsepower. Generally speaking, the larger pieces of machinery and equipment come under the unified management of the communes or production brigades, which makes it possible to concentrate technical forces, carry out unified deployment, raise utilization ratios and economize on manpower and materials.

2. Unified disposition of basic construction for farmland water conservancy. Thirty years of agricultural development in China has taught us that farmland capital construction projects and improvements in production conditions in agriculture require the concerted efforts of an entire commune or of several communes. During this period 84,000 reservoirs with a total capacity of 400 billion cubic meters were built, as well as 2.1 million motor- and electrically-pumped wells with conveyance systems and a considerable number of fields producing high and stable yields. While some of these projects were built by the state, a good many of them were built by the people themselves with the communes playing an active role.

3. Setting up commune- and brigade-run enterprises. There are now about 1.36 million such enterprises in the countryside, of which 337,800 are run by people's communes, or an average of 6.2 per commune. Ninety-eight percent of the communes throughout China run their own enterprises. Some 31.13 million people, or 18 percent of the total labor force in the people's communes, are engaged in commune- and brigade-run industries. Of these, 18 million, or 66.6 percent of the workers in such enterprises, are engaged in industry. In 1982, the gross income of commune- and brigade-run enterprises amounted to 77 billion yuan. In 1979, the gross value of output was 64 billion, or 11.6 percent of China's gross value of industrial production. These enterprises now occupy a substantial position in the national economy.

4. Building residential centers. With commune members living in relatively compact communities, it became easier to make unified plans for education, science, sports, health and hygiene, and thus offer the peasants a richer and more varied life.

There is now considerable discussion about the commune's combining government administration and economic management. It is generally felt that this system is disadvantageous to the commune's exercising autonomy as a production unit. China's 1982 constitution affirms the principle of separating government administration from economic management. The question now is how economic management is to be carried out in the future. Experiments are now being made in a number of provinces and regions. These will provide experience for seeking forms of management beneficial to the development of China's rural economy and better adapting the management system of the collective economy to the development of the productive forces in the countryside.

9. Evaluation of the Movement for Agricultural Collectivization

Experience has shown that collectivization has promoted the advance of agriculture and benefited the development of the national economy as a whole. As regards the ideology guiding this movement, general understanding of the issues involved has deepened in the course of practice.

As early as 1953, the Central Committee of the Chinese Communist Party pointed out in its "Decision on Mutual Aid and Cooperation in Agricultural Production":

> The Central Committee of the Chinese Communist Party has always upheld the notion that in order to overcome many of the difficulties encountered by the masses of peasants engaged in decentralized management, as well as to enable the greater number of poor peasants to develop production quickly and obtain sufficient food and clothing, to bring about great increases in manufactured products, grain and raw materials above present levels, to increase the purchasing power of the peasants, and to expand the market for goods manufactured in China, it is necessary to promote the concept of "organization", and to develop the positive aspects of mutual aid and cooperation on a voluntary basis. At present, this form of mutual aid and cooperation is founded upon collective labor which is based on the individual economy (based on the peasants' private property), and will develop eventually into agricultural collectivization or socialism.

In his report "On the Cooperative Transformation of Agriculture" delivered in July 1955 on the eve of the upsurge of the movement for the cooperative transformation of agriculture, Mao Zedong wrote:

> China's current level of production of commodity grain and raw materials for industry is low, whereas the state's need for them is growing year by year, and this presents a sharp contradiction. If we cannot . . . solve the problem of agricultural cooperation . . . , that is to say, if our agriculture cannot make a leap from small-scale farming with animal-drawn farm implements to large-scale mechanized farming, along with extensive state-organized land reclamation by settlers using machinery . . . , then we shall fail to resolve the contradiction between the ever-increasing need for commodity grain and industrial raw materials and the present generally low output of staple crops, and we shall run into formidable difficulties in our socialist industrialization and be unable to complete it.

The above quotations show that the Party and government were from the very outset clearly aware that the cooperative transformation of agriculture was to serve the national economy as a whole, and thus paid close attention to developing the forces of production in the agricultural economy as well as encouraged the increase of marketable farm products. It was subsequently shown that the cooperative transformation of agriculture made gains. It increased the degree of socialization in production, gave powerful support to socialist economic construction, and thus attained its objectives. This indicates that the principle of agricultural collectivization, as well as the thinking behind the principle, were both valid. But there were shortcomings, which began to manifest themselves mainly in the final stages of the cooperative movement in agriculture: Wishful thinking born of overimpatience to achieve results interfered with the laws of development of the movement itself. After the summer of 1955, insufficient guidance was given to peasants who were in too much of a hurry to set up cooperatives, so that work in this respect was done too hastily and carelessly and manifested a tendency toward oversimplification and uniformity. Furthermore, the "upsurge" disrupted the original schedule which called for setting up cooperatives over a period of 15 years, and the transition from individual to collective economy was achieved in only three years. The peasants' right to individual ownership was abolished too early — before the elementary cooperatives had had time to develop fully. This left problems in some districts, causing difficulties in the subsequent task of consolidating the cooperatives.

On the whole, however, the cooperative movement progressed satisfactorily. The problems that remained were adequately dealt with by follow-up work.

The most serious problems started during the so-called "Great Leap Forward". The preposterous targets, the "communist wind" and a series of arbitrary and impractical directives caused grave damage to agricultural production. Gross value of agricultural output, which had reached 53.7 billion yuan in 1957, dropped 24.6 percent to 40.5 billion yuan in 1961 (calculated according to the fixed prices of 1957). This was even lower than the figure for 1952. In other words, the Great Leap Forward set China's agriculture back ten years.

The reasons for this disaster are as follows:

1. The difficulty, complexity and extended nature of the work of transforming the small peasant economy were poorly understood, and the movement to set up people's communes was launched nationwide without seeking experience from pilot projects. In the theoretical realm, there was an overevaluation of the achievements of the cooperative movement and failure to take into account the excessive haste of the later stage of that movement. A subjective desire to replace collective ownership with ownership by the whole people also manifested itself, as well as negation of the principle of equal exchange in the relations between the state and the peasant and among the collectives, so that the necessary economic interests were either neglected or encroached upon.

2. The principle of combining progress with consolidation

was disregarded, and an attempt was made to replace the law of "progress — consolidation — progress" with the concept of "rapid and uninterrupted progress". The major task after the cooperative movement was to perfect a management system, and to this end much effort should have been devoted to building up and consolidating the communes' infrastructure, setting up and perfecting responsibility systems and the system of payment according to work done, promoting agricultural research and popularizing its results, stimulating the development of the productive forces, and making rational use of the manpower, materials, funds and natural resources of the collective economy to bring in the best possible economic results. But the desire to constantly raise the degree of public ownership became an obsession, and the work of consolidation was forgotten.

3. There was insufficient respect for the right of the collective agricultural economies to run their own affairs, nor was sufficient attention paid to managing the collective economy by economic means. Specifically, the latter manifested itself as excessive administrative interference and inappropriate handling of the relations between the state, the collective and the individual, so that the state's interests were often stressed at the expense of those of the collective and the individual. If the system that combined government administration with economic management had been correctly integrated with democratic management, the grass-roots organs of political power (i.e., the people's communes) would have had a broader democratic footing and political power would have served to enhance people's democracy. But as it was the system merely became a means of increasing administrative intervention.

These shortcomings and errors were later rectified as the people's commune system underwent further development. Under Party and government leadership, the "communist wind", inflated claims, arbitrary methods of leadership and the setting of excessively high targets were criticized; unrealistic attitudes with regard to communism and providing "to each according to his needs" were rectified; and the three-level management system was established. These measures returned agricultural development to the correct path. Between 1963 and 1965, three years were spent readjusting the production relations in agriculture. With a greater sense of reassurance among the peasants, agricultural production made fresh advances. In these three years agriculture advanced fairly rapidly: By 1965, gross output value had surpassed that of 1957, reaching 59 billion yuan in terms of 1957 prices. The peasants' income from distribution was also somewhat higher than in 1957.

This is evidence of the vitality of the socialist collective-ownership economy. Although its shortcomings were many and varied, they did not result in a vicious circle but were instead swiftly corrected through reliance on the collective economy.

Chapter IV

THE AGRICULTURAL ECONOMY
DURING THE TEN YEARS OF TURMOIL

The "cultural revolution" which began in 1966 was a disastrous period of turmoil that deeply affected China's politics, economy, culture and society. People have rightly called this period the "ten catastrophic years". The damage it caused was more than superficial; it left internal wounds which are more serious and often take longer to heal than external ones. Such "internal" injuries refer to ideological and psychological traumas, rather than material and economic losses.

The ten years of turmoil also caused serious damage in the rural economy, the area most deeply affected being that of policy thinking. Lin Biao and the Gang of Four were experts at using revolutionary terminology to spread reactionary sophistry. At a time when China's socialist revolution was completed, when the collective rural economy had been consolidated, and when fundamental changes had been effected in rural class relations, they mendaciously claimed that China's countryside was threatened by a resurgence of the landlord and bourgeois classes, and in all seriousness announced the existence of a sharp struggle between "two classes, two roads and two lines" in the rural economy. Using the media to deceive the masses, they labeled many socialist systems of management and normal productive activities as bourgeois and capitalist, thus causing serious damage to the collective economy.

The first thing they stigmatized as belonging to the "capitalist road" was the commodity and currency economy. In the eyes of the Gang of Four, commodities and money were products of the capitalist system and were doomed to perish together with that system. They scorned all economic laws and denied that the law of value — basic to a commodity economy — had any function in a socialist economy. They proposed administrative means as the sole method of managing the economy. They used the three-level management system of the people's communes for their own ends. They turned the system of democratic management from below into a tool for ruling from above. In his notorious article "On Proletarian Dictatorship", the Gang's master strategist, Zhang Chunqiao, went so far as to list peasants and other small producers as the targets of proletarian dictatorship. Actually, the proletarian dictatorship they referred to was not proletarian at all; it was purely and simply a fascist dictatorship. They distorted Lenin's notion that "small production daily and hourly generated capitalism" in the Russian countryside before the victory of the socialist revolution (before the collectivization of agriculture), and mistakenly called this an "inherent characteristic" of small production. Thus with one fell swoop they drove the peasantry into the bourgeois camp and relegated them to the status of enemies of socialist revolution. The Gang touted a feudal-fascist economic regime under which the peasants were slaves tied down to the land they worked without the possibility of emancipation.

Since the commodity economy was seen as capitalist, everything connected with it was banned — cost, profits and economic accounting were all taboo. The Gang declared: "We must keep political, not economic, accounts" and "Better to grow socialist weeds than capitalist shoots". To them, enterprise losses were insignificant. With such thinking dominating the economic scene, little respect was left for the labor of the peasant masses; arbitrary and impractical directives as well neglect for cost accounting and economic returns reduced much of it to ineffectual labor. Once the commune economy ceased to be a commodity economy, it inevitably came within the orbit of a fascist economy. Economic exploitation was accompanied by extra-economic oppression and persecution.

The Gang of Four maintained that instead of concentration on production the main duty of the production team was to implement "dictatorship" (real fascist dictatorship over the peasants), and that its main activity should therefore be class struggle. Anyone attempting to do otherwise would risk being accused of pursuing the "theory of the unique importance of the productive forces". As a result, agricultural production was gravely affected, and it was only due to resistance on the part of the peasants and rural cadres that the rural economy managed to maintain a low level of development.

What the Gang of Four referred to as the "theory of the unique importance of the productive forces" was a thoroughly anti-Marxist concoction. It is common knowledge that all human activity must be based on some form of economic activity or else it becomes "a flower without roots and a river without a source". The Gang had a sinister motive in fabricating this so-called "theory of the unique importance of the productive forces". Their intention was to use such criticism to validate their philosophy of "struggle, struggle and struggle". They clamored that China's socialist countryside was a hotbed of class struggle teeming with new landlord and bourgeois elements, and that in certain districts and departments the latter had already seized power and set up their own dictatorships. The aim of such lurid propaganda was to prepare public opinion for a takeover of Party and state power by the "Leftists" — as they styled themselves. These careerists plotted to place China under their control.

Another club used by the Gang to disrupt the rural economy was the so-called presence of "bourgeois rights". By calling for the repudiation of such "bourgeois rights", they attempted to create ideological confusion and sabotage the system of distribution according to work. Distorting the theories of Marxism, they applied Marx's comparison of the distribution systems of the two stages of communism (i.e., socialism and communism) to the distribution systems of socialism and capitalism — two entirely different social systems, and labeled "distribution according to work" a bourgeois form of distribution. Their purpose in vilifying the socialist system of distribution was to institute a system wherein everyone's share of the distribution was more or less the same; in other words, an egalitarian system of distribution. People have called this "eating from the same big pot", meaning that every person received the same remuneration regardless of his or her contribution to the collective economy. The net result was to smother the masses' initiative for production. Zhang Chunqiao went so far as to advocate instituting a wartime "rations system" in times of peace, praising this system for embodying the spirit of communism. Such a view was, of course, utterly absurd and unscientific and had nothing in common with scientific communism.

In addition to spreading various absurd "Leftist" theories, the Gang of Four used the power they had usurped to carry out a set of preposterous "Leftist" policies with the following objectives:

1.   Establishing one-crop agriculture. This was one of the most outstanding features of the Gang's economic thinking, and it dovetailed with their political concept of practicing "dictatorship" over the peasants. In their view, peasants needed only a modicum of food and clothing, and for that it was only necessary to have grain. They did their best to advocate asceticism, while they themselves reveled in luxury. They had certain districts grow special produce for their own enjoyment, but cared little if the peasants starved. Distorting the principle put forward by the Party and government of "taking grain as the key link and striving for all-round development", they in effect advocated "taking grain as the only crop and chopping down everything else". They did all they could to prevent diversification of the rural economy. Not only was the running of such industries as brick kilns and transportation services considered heretical and thus banned; even the management of fruit orchards, tea plantations, fish ponds and reed ponds was regarded as improper. Such stupidities as draining lakes and ponds, building dykes in the sea, cutting down forests and destroying pastureland in order to reclaim land for planting grain ended up causing inestimable damage to forestry, animal husbandry and fishery. Grave imbalances appeared in the rural economy and the natural ecology.

2. Indiscriminate transfer of resources belonging to the rural production units. In the economic thinking of the Gang of Four, such concepts as "equal exchange" and "compensation for value" did not exist. Essentially upholders of the feudal system, they in fact modeled their agricultural economics on the practices of the former serfowners, who held to the principle that "everything under heaven belongs to the sovereign". Thus the Gang felt they could dispose of the peasants' property as they pleased. They legalized the so-called "transfers" — an erroneous practice which had originated during the Great Leap Forward and was later rectified. These "transfers" took many forms, both direct and indirect. The production teams' funds, materials and labor power were "transferred" without payment to construct unnecessary and extravagant buildings. Labor was requisitioned to build non-productive projects for county and commune administrations. Funds provided by the state for education, health and communications were diverted for other uses, and the burden of paying for these undertakings was shifted onto the production teams. Farmland capital construction was carried on blindly with no consideration of its feasibility, so that the production teams' labor power would be tied down for long periods of time. Materials were "bought" from the production teams at ridiculously low prices. Exactions were made from the salaries of employees in enterprises run by communes and brigades. All these practices caused unwarranted economic losses to the production teams. An investigation made in the Hongtang Commune of Xiangxiang County, Hunan Province shows that in the heyday of Lin Biao and the Gang of Four such extraneous burdens gradually increased until they covered more than 70 items in 20 different fields, and amounted to 40 percent or more of the commune members' yearly income from distribution.

Another drain on the peasants' resources was bloated administrations and unnecessarily large numbers of cadres in the production teams. An investigation made in Fujian Province shows that, in addition to the principal cadres in the production teams, there were ten categories of administrative personnel:

accountants, assistant accountants, cashiers, clerks, storekeepers, radio announcers, weather observers, information officers, persons in charge of cooperative medicare, and administrators of culture and education. In addition, there were teachers who taught in schools run by the production teams and the "barefoot doctors". Besides their own regular workpoints, the peasants had to provide the subsidiary workpoints for all these people.

3. "Cutting off the tail of capitalism". The peasants planted private plots and engaged in household sidelines under a long-established system called "small freedoms within the big collective". When interference by Lin Biao and the Gang of Four reached its extremes, however, these activities were regarded as "tails of capitalism" which had to be "cut off", and on this basis, a grand variety of queer rules and regulations were drawn up. For instance, each household was allowed to raise only three chickens; any more than that was "capitalism". In some places it was decreed that the number of chickens was not to exceed the number of people in the household, and any chickens above that figure were confiscated. In some places, commune members were forbidden to gather wild plants in the mountains, or to plant trees around their houses. Lists of what animals the commune members could not raise and what things they could not plant or gather were circulated in the form of general orders. Such incidents were legion and aroused great resentment among the peasants.

4. Banning country fairs. Since commune members were forbidden to engage in sideline production, it was all the more difficult for them to hold country fairs. The well-known Haertao country fair in Liaoning Province was described as a "bastion for the restoration of capitalism" and in need of "reform". In Anhui Province, a large-scale campaign to "revolutionize commerce" was conducted, with armed men "mopping up" the country fairs. In order to thoroughly eradicate the fairs, chicken-raising was banned and the peasants' sheep and goats were slaughtered, or else vegetables and melon vines in the peasants'

private plots were eradicated. Such outrageous acts seriously damaged normal economic life in the countryside.

5. "Transition in poverty". This was another of the absurd policies pursued by the Gang of Four. Their argument was that the poorer the people, the more revolutionary they are, and thus transition to communism should be carried out while the people are still poor. Guided by such "policy" thinking, many production teams "transitioned" (went over) to ownership by the production brigade before conditions were ripe. This in effect meant forcibly evening out economic disparities between the production teams — in other words, egalitarianism. At one stage, when the "wind of transition" movement was at its height, entire districts and provinces went over to ownership by the production brigade. This gravely damaged the enthusiasm of the commune members and caused great harm to agricultural and sideline production.

Due to frequent changes in policy, teams which had not yet been "transitioned" did not know what to expect and simply drifted along. They did not plan for the future, refused to buy large draft animals or farm implements, no longer engaged in farmland capital construction, and refused to build more houses or plant more trees for fear that a sudden "transition" would deprive them of the fruit of their efforts. Some brigades and teams hurriedly slaughtered all their pigs and sheep and chopped down their trees as soon as news of a possible "transition" reached their ears. Some teams surreptitiously divided up their property and sold all their assets. Such acts naturally had the effect of seriously damaging the agricultural forces of production.

Wherever the "wind of transition" blew, communes and brigades were amalgamated, allegedly to prevent "polarization" from taking place among them. Thus, the communes and brigades kept increasing in size. In 1965, there were 74,755 communes and 5,412,000 brigades throughout the country, but by 1970, their numbers had declined to 51,478 and 4,564,000 respectively. The brigades increased in size from 25 households each on the average to 32.6, and the proportion of communes with brigades as the accounting unit rose from 5 percent in 1962 to 14 percent in 1970.

The ideological system of the Gang of Four's ultra-"Left" line was fundamentally metaphysical and formalistic. What, in their view, was most revolutionary and "socialistic"? They apparently believed that the larger the economic unit and the higher the degree of public ownership the better. They ignored the fact that socialism is a mode of production, that each mode of production is founded on relations of production, and that specific relations of production are determined by specific forces of production. The ultra-"Left" policies the Gang promoted in the agricultural economy not only played havoc with agricultural production, but also created indescribable confusion in people's minds.

During the ten years of turmoil, the movement to "Learn from Dazhai" was used by the Gang of Four for their own ends.

Dazhai refers to a particular production brigade in the Dazhai Commune in Xiyang County, Shanxi Province. Nature had not been kind to this brigade: most of its land lined the slopes of a rocky hill behind the village, and the rest, in the form of accumulated layers of silt, was scattered in a number of deep gullies. The soil was thin, and the fields small. Some 700 *mu* of farmland was broken up into more than 4,700 plots, the largest no bigger than 5 *mu*. After a cooperative was set up here in 1953, per *mu* yields of grain rose somewhat, although not much above 100 *jin*, and poverty was still an ever-present reality. The peasants decided to turn the land on the slopes into level fields by relying on the strength of the collective economy. Dams were built across the ravines to prevent the soil from being washed away by rain, and the 4,700 plots of land were transformed into 1,800 high- and stable-yield fields. Grain harvests rose steadily to more than 800 *jin* per *mu*. The peasants had worked a miracle — and they were rightly praised for it. In 1964, Mao Zedong put forward the slogan "Learn from Dazhai", and at the First Session of the Third National People's Congress held in December of the same year, Zhou Enlai lauded Dazhai in his Report on the Work of the Government. Zhou summarized the main principles at work: placing politics in command and ideology in the lead; love for the country and the collective; and self-reliance and hard struggle. From then on, a nationwide movement to "Learn from Dazhai" swept the Chinese countryside.

After the "cultural revolution" began in 1966, Dazhai fell into the clutches of the Gang of Four. Taking advantage of Dazhai's reputation, the Gang first implemented ultra-"Left" agricultural policies, and then spread them throughout the country by means of the movement to "Learn from Dazhai". The actual experiences of the Dazhai production brigade were entirely disregarded. Dazhai came to represent the ultra-"Left" line in the countryside and during the "cultural revolution" functioned as a model and propagator of that line — against the will of the people of Dazhai.

Chapter V

RURAL ECONOMIC POLICY IN THE NEW PERIOD

1. Point of Departure

The Third Plenary Session of the Eleventh Central Committee of the Chinese Communist Party was held at the end of 1978, two years after the fall of the Gang of Four. Proceeding from a correct Marxist line, the participants at this plenary session exposed the disruptive counterrevolutionary activities of the Gang of Four, thoroughly repudiated their "Left" errors in forms of theory, ideology and policy, and pointed out the dangers they represented. The session decided to shift the focus of all work onto socialist modernization beginning in 1979, thus opening a new page in China's history.

In September 1979, the Fourth Plenary Session of the Party's Eleventh Central Committee passed the "Decisions on a Number of Questions Related to the Speeding Up of Agricultural Development". It summed up the development and *status quo* of China's rural economy and made many specific stipulations with regard to rural economic policy.

The primary point of departure of the new rural economic policies was to give full play to the superiority of the socialist system and to the initiative of China's 800 million peasants, to pay close attention to material benefits for the peasant masses on the economic plane and, on the political plane, to provide real guarantees for the peasants' democratic rights.

In order to implement these new policies, it was imperative for the whole nation to reach a common understanding on matters related to agriculture. The basis of this understanding consisted of the following points:

(1) A political situation of stability and unity is a necessary condition for agriculture to flourish. Agriculture is the basis of China's economy, but for agriculture to fulfill this role and create the proper conditions for gradually realizing China's modernization program, there must be an extended period of political stability.

(2) The question of class struggle in the countryside has to be dealt with correctly. Enormous changes have taken place in the economic and social structures in the Chinese countryside since the cooperative movement took place in the 1950s. The landlord class has been eliminated as a class and there are only a small number of class enemies in the countryside who view the socialist system with hostility and try to disrupt it. Although it is incorrect to overlook the class struggle in the countryside, it is equally wrong to exaggerate its existence and describe it as ubiquitous and ever-present, since such an attitude is bound to magnify the scope of struggle to the detriment of stability and unity. A lesson learned from past "Leftist" mistakes is that it is incorrect to confuse contradictions among the people with those against the enemy. It is even worse to magnify or fabricate situations of "class struggle". Erroneous thinking and behavior among peasants should be dealt with by patient persuasion and education to help these peasants change their ways on their own accord.

(3) The socialist education of the peasants should be carried out correctly so as to avoid interference from either the "Left" or the Right. Various phenomena appearing in the course of the development of the agricultural economy should be viewed in a correct light. It is especially important to differentiate correctly between what is socialist and what is capitalist. The Gang of Four vastly expanded the scope of things labeled capitalist out of their own ulterior motives; their aim was actually to negate socialist phenomena by stigmatizing them as capitalist. The after-effects of such practices must be eradicat-

ed. Problems in the agricultural sector should be handled in a sober and realistic manner.

(4) All work should be handled in a realistic manner and in line with the laws of nature and economics. It is entirely wrong to base the management of agriculture on wishful thinking and to disregard realities, ignore the democratic rights of commune members and issue administrative orders indiscriminately. Above all, the democratic rights of the peasants should be respected, and they should be consulted in all matters related to their interests. Only in this way can agricultural construction be placed on a realistic footing and be carried forward.

The above points are the basis of the common understanding needed for agricultural work in the new period as well as the point of departure for a series of new policies for the rural economy.

2. Policies on Price Readjustment and Financial Credits and Loans

After more than 30 years of development, China's rural economy has by and large rid itself of the limitations of a natural economy, and a commodity economy has grown up around it. Observance of the law of value is a prerequisite for economic advance. And if this law is to be observed in the rural economy, equitable price parities must be maintained between industrial and agricultural products and among different agricultural products, so that exchanges of these products can be conducted on the basis of equal or approximately equal value. This will ensure that workers, peasants and other people engaged in production enjoy equitable economic benefits and maintain cooperation and division of labor among themselves.

Before Liberation, irrational price parities had long existed in China between agricultural and industrial products. Industry exploited agriculture and the cities exploited the countryside. Since Liberation, the government has paid considerable attention to price readjustment so as to ensure rural development and protect the peasants' interests. Statistics show that the rate of exchange of agricultural produce for industrial goods was 30 percent lower in the late 1940s than it was prior to the outbreak of the War of Resistance Against Japanese Aggression in 1937, and that the scissors gap had enlarged about 34 percent. As a result of readjustments in price parities after Liberation, state purchase prices for agricultural products in 1952 rose 21.6 percent over those in 1950, while retail prices for rural-use industrial goods rose by only 9.7 percent in the same period. The exchange price differential between agricultural and industrial products decreased 9.7 percent at an average annual rate of 5 percent. In the 10 years from 1953 to 1962 during the First and Second Five-Year Plans, purchase prices of agricultural products rose 61 percent, retail prices for rural-use industrial products rose 14.7 percent, and the exchange price differential fell another 29.2 percent at an average rate of 3.4 percent annually. In the 16 years between 1962 and 1978, the government intended to continue implementing a policy of reducing the exchange price differential, but owing to the serious damage caused by the ten years of turmoil beginning in 1966 and the drying up of China's financial resources, the policy was discontinued. In these 16 years, the purchase price for agricultural produce and byproducts rose only 7.5 percent, retail prices for rural-use industrial goods decreased 12.3 percent, and the exchange price differential between industrial and agricultural products narrowed by 18.9 percent at an average annual rate of 1.3 percent. Thus comparing 1978 figures with those of 1950, the purchase prices of farm sideline products throughout China rose by about 107.3 percent, retail prices of rural-use industrial products rose 9.8 percent, and the exchange price differential between industrial and agricultural products decreased by about 47 percent. Based on 1952 prices, the increase in the peasants' cash incomes due to such factors as rises in purchase prices for farm and sideline products, negotiated-price purchases, and higher prices for above-quota purchases of grain and oilseeds amounted to some 133 billion yuan after making allowances for rises in the retail prices of industrial goods bought by the peasants. This gave the peasants an average net benefit of 5.1 billion yuan per year and did much to improve living standards in the countryside and promote agricultural advances. But prices cannot be divorced from value. In the 21 years between 1957 and 1978, labor productivity in industry throughout the country rose 75 percent, while in agriculture it increased only 15 percent. The result was a marked drop in the value per unit of industrial products and a rise in that of farm and sideline products. If the price parities between industrial and agricultural products are viewed in this context, it is obvious that exchange prices for agricultural and industrial products had become more irrational, rather than the opposite. This was due to the fact that the state's financial capabilities declined during the ten years of the "cultural revolution" and it was unable to raise the prices for farm and sideline products.

After the downfall of the Gang of Four — especially after the Party's Third Plenary Session — the government adopted an important economic policy: beginning in 1979, the purchase price of 18 major farm and sideline products was raised by a considerable margin. Starting from the grain harvest in the summer of 1979, state monopoly purchase price for grain was raised 20 percent, and on this basis another 50 percent was paid for above-quota purchases. Thus the average purchase price for six types of state-controlled grain (wheat, rice, soybeans, maize, millet and sorghum) rose from 10.64 yuan to 12.86 yuan per 100 *jin*, a 20.86 percent increase. The state-monopoly purchase price for cotton was raised an average of 15 percent throughout the country, with another 30 percent added for above-quota purchases. An additional subsidy of 5 percent was given in most places in northern China where the output of cotton per unit of land is low and the benefits from planting it are small. The purchase prices of fats and oilseeds rose by an average of 25 percent, with a 50 percent addition for above-quota purchases. The purchase price was raised 26 percent for hogs, and between 20 and 50 percent for beef cattle, sheep (for mutton), sugar beets, sugarcane, hemp, jute, silkworm cocoons,

Irrigation converts once-barren lands in northern Jiangsu Province into fertile fields.

Trimming poplars —
effort in Cangxian C

Liu Anqin
incubator —
ship in the c

A commune-operated blanket factory
in Weihai, Shandong Province.

Mechanized tank for raising fish, Wuxian County, Jiangsu.

f the afforestation

his wife at their family
ample of private entrepreneur-
-raising field.

Private florists in Shanghai.

Sheep herding on the rich pastures of Inner Mongolia.

New housing for the farmers of Yantai, Shandong.

aquatic products, cow hides, water buffalo hides, timber and *mao* bamboo. For eggs, the purchase rose by an average of 30 percent, and by 8.2 percent for honey.

This rise in prices was the largest since Liberation, with the overall index of purchase prices for farm and sideline products throughout the country in 1979 rising by 22.1 percent over that in 1978. The state disbursed 10.8 billion yuan for this price hike, which contributed to both narrowing the price gap between industrial and agricultural products and promoting agricultural production. It resulted in the peasants earning an additional 7.8 billion yuan that year.

Meanwhile, the principle of combining regulation by planning with market regulation was implemented with regard to pricing policy. Under this principle, the system of negotiated prices for purchasing and selling third-category farm and sideline products, once practiced in the country, was restored. And in a number of places the system was applied to the purchase and sale of such first-category products as grain and oil crops and a number of second-category products on the condition that the state purchase quotas were first fulfilled. This measure made up for deficiencies in state planning, increased market supplies and livened up the rural economy.

Controlling prices is a highly complicated matter. When drawing up and implementing price policies, the state must consider not only price parities between industrial and agricultural products, but also parities among agricultural products themselves. This includes price parities among the major grain crops, between grain and various cash crops, and between grain and cash crops and animal husbandry products. Maintaining rational relationships between these parities is essential for the all-round development of agriculture. The state has done much work toward this end. Between 1950 and 1979, for example, the price of rice was raised on nine occasions, that of wheat raised on nine occasions and lowered on four occasions, that of cotton raised on 12 occasions and lowered on five occasions, and that of hogs raised on 23 occasions and lowered twice. And it is in line with the above principle that prices of farm and sideline products were raised by a large margin in 1979, and that further adjustments were made in the price of farm products in 1980.

In implementing price policies, price differences between one region and another were also taken into consideration. Relations between adjacent regions were dealt with first. In this way, price fluctuations for the same farm product due to a lack of unity in pricing methods, quality standards and the time of effecting price readjustments could be avoided. In its handling of regional price differences, the state regulates the supply of goods between regions by rationally fixing prices in line with the normal flow of commodities, thus protecting the interests of both the producer and the consumer.

After adjusting the prices of 18 farm and sideline products in 1979, the state has also raised by 10 to 30 percent the purchase prices of cotton, jute, tung oil, resin, gutta-percha, timber, goatskins, sheepskins and medicinal herbs.

Furthermore, the state has defined guidelines and policies for assisting agricultural development through the medium of finances and credits and loans. These guidelines envisage gradually raising the proportion of agriculture-related investment in the entire investment for capital construction within three to five years. Generally speaking, state finance funds for agriculture have tended to increase due to the government's constant emphasis on this branch of the economy. Between 1952 and 1979, such funds increased 18.1 times, from 900 million yuan to 17,180 million yuan. The annual proportion of state investment in agriculture as against the gross output value from agriculture in the same year also saw a gradual increase. In 1952, such investment was 583 million yuan, or 1.2 percent of that year's gross value of agricultural output (48,400 million yuan); in 1957, 1,187 million yuan, or 2 percent of the gross value of agricultural output (60,400 million yuan); in 1965, 2,497 million yuan, or 4.2 percent of the gross value of agricultural output (59,000 million yuan); and in 1979, 5,792 million yuan, or 3.7 percent of the gross value of agricultural output for that year (158,400 million yuan). These proportions are low compared to other countries. The new policy envisages raising the proportion of investment for agriculture to about 18 percent of the entire investment for capital construction, and the proportion of funds for agricultural undertakings and assistance to communes and brigades to about 8 percent of the state's gross expenditure. The income of local administrations is to be used mainly for agriculture and agriculture-related industry. Investment in agriculture will thereby take up a much larger proportion of the gross value of output from agriculture. With a view to assisting underdeveloped regions, the state established a "Development Fund for Underdeveloped Regions" in 1980. This fund spends 500 million yuan annually for construction in mountainous, outlying and minority-nationality regions to speed up their economic development.

Regarding credits and loans, bank loans to agriculture will increase in amount. Meanwhile, the state is issuing special long-term, low-interest loans. In 1979, the Agricultural Bank resumed its operation with an end to strengthen rural credit and loan undertakings. The bank specializes in nationwide rural financial work. Its basic mission is to exercise unified management over funds for agriculture, handle rural credits and loans, give leadership to rural credit cooperatives, and develop banking in the rural areas. Credit cooperatives have long existed in the Chinese countryside, playing an important role in the rural economy. By the end of 1979, there were roughly 59,000 credit cooperatives throughout China and about 350,000 credit stations. Their deposits, totaling 21,600 million yuan, were used as loans to aid rural communes and brigades. The new economic policies call for improving the distribution of rural credits and loans, constantly reforming and perfecting the credit and loan system, respecting the rights of credit and loan cooperatives to make their own decisions, and getting the cooperatives to play a more important role in bolstering the rural economy.

3. Respecting the Right of Production Teams to Decide Their Own Affairs

In the three-level system of administration implemented in the people's communes, manpower, land, farming implements and draft animals are permanently managed by the production teams, which serve also as production and distribution units. Now these teams manage their production and finances with a direct bearing on the interests of every team member.

There would be no point in raising the matter of respecting the production teams' rights to decide their own affairs if these rights had never been infringed upon. The fact is that these rights were encroached upon for a considerable length of time, a state of affairs which has aroused a good deal of attention.

As a result of the production teams' inability to manage their own affairs, agricultural production has very often become divorced from actual local conditions. A case in point is the matter of planting double-crop rice in Sichuan Province. Sichuan is a large province with a varied terrain of mountains, hills and plains. Temperatures, rainfall and frost-free periods vary from county to county. Thus farm production is bound to suffer if it is managed at the provincial, district or even county level. But in the heyday of the Gang of Four, double-cropping of rice was promoted throughout the province and caused great discontent among the peasants. After the downfall of the Gang, provincial leaders went to investigate the situation in the countryside and found that in many places double-cropping was unfeasible owing to shortages of manpower and fertilizer and the brevity of the planting season. They decided that farming should reflect local conditions and that production teams should determine their own affairs. The peasants' enthusiasm for production rose considerably. At present, many problems of this nature remain unsolved. Thus the policy of allowing production teams to exercise full rights of decision over all important matters related to production must be further publicized.

Such decisions involve more than farming according to local

conditions. They also are concerned with management planning, land use, crop disposition and planting seasons, employment of labor power, management of materials and distribution of finances — none of which can be done properly if the production teams' rights of decision are not respected. Take for instance the Gaoxigou Brigade in Mizhi County, Shaanxi Province. Situated on a loess plateau, its 3,000 *mu* of cultivated land spreads over 43 hills and 21 gullies. Serious soil erosion and frequent natural disasters resulted in poor harvests for nine out of ten years and made life extremely difficult for the local peasants. After 1957, people there began to rearrange their production programs in the light of the local environment and ecology, thereby gaining some positive results. But these achievements were wiped out when the "cultural revolution" began. After 1971, production picked up again, but only to a limited extent. It was only when the policy of respecting the production teams' rights to make their own decisions was implemented that they took the strategic step of allocating farmland to planting trees and grass. While improving crop cultivation, they also put much effort into developing forestry and animal husbandry, with spectacular results. Farming, forestry and animal husbandry now each account for one-third of the agricultural economy; water and soil conservation has considerably improved; and the soil is better able to retain moisture. Grain production has risen from about 100 *jin* per *mu* in 1957 to more than 600 *jin*. This, plus the teams' income from forestry and animal husbandry, has greatly ameliorated the team members' financial circumstances.

Implementation of the policy of respecting the production teams' rights to decide their own affairs has met with considerable resistance, most stemming from the influence of ultra-"Leftist" thinking. For a long time many people in the agricultural sector believed that agriculture in a socialist country must be operated on a large scale with a high degree of public ownership; in fact, the "larger" and the more "public" the better. The tendency was for the people's communes to control and direct all matters related to production, while the production teams obeyed orders and had no right to make decisions. In actual work, the stress was on unified action — unified plans for planting, unified working hours, unified requirements for plowing, and unified specifications for farm work. Many fancy schemes were devised with regard to the management of labor power to prove the advantages of "large" and "public" agriculture, principally transferring able-bodied workers from the production teams and organizing them into commune-led work brigades for capital construction projects. As a consequence, farm production suffered setbacks because the production teams lacked sufficient manpower. Such thinking engendered the main resistance to the new policy. It became clear that people's thinking had to be set straight before the policy could be implemented.

In a sense, implementing the policy of respect for the production teams' rights of decision constitutes a revolution. This is because ultra-"Leftist" thinking has also affected the style of work of government cadres. Reports from Henan Province reveal that during the time of the Gang of Four, some county administrations, in order to get the peasants to plant rice and "unify cultivation", compelled the latter to pull up their tobacco plants and plow under their sweet potatoes. They even promoted such absurd slogans as "Divorce yourselves from sorghum", "Disown sweet potatoes" and "Exterminate beans". In Gansu Province, some county administrations ordered all pear, persimmom and walnut trees — trees that were already full-grown and bearing fruit — cut down in line with the slogan "Send fruit trees up into the mountains". Some counties insisted that the sowing of all wheat should take place at the same time, and even sent out work teams to ensure that this was done. In such places there was of course no question of respecting the rights of the production teams to decide their own affairs.

The question of respecting the rights of the production teams to decide their own affairs, raised at the Third Plenary Session of the Party's Central Committee, is identical in principle to that of respecting the rights of enterprises in industrial departments to decide their own affairs, a question raised at the same time. Involved here is also the matter of how to manage a socialist enterprise. Management of industrial enterprises in China shared common defects with management in agricultural departments — both suffered from overconcentration of power, which fettered the enthusiasm and initiative of grass-roots production units and hampered the development of the economy. In agriculture, respecting the rights of production teams to decide their own affairs means that the production team, if it accepts the guidance of state planning, has the right to manage farming in the light of its own conditions, to make decisions concerning raising production, to choose methods of administration and management, and to distribute its own products and cash. It also has the right to disregard arbitrary directives from any leader or leading organization. These rights — of production, disposition, management and administration, and distribution — have been called the "four big rights". Some people include the right to disregard incorrect directives and call them the "five big rights".

The people's commune is an economic organization based on collective ownership, in which all activities should be based on decisions of its own membership. It should practice democracy and democratic administration, otherwise the term "collective ownership" could hardly apply to it. In this sense, the formulation "respect the right of the production team to decide its own affairs" does not fully express the essence of the matter. A well-rounded exposition would have to include the matter of the production team's right of ownership. Thus, the communique of the Third Plenary Session of the Eleventh Central Committee of the Communist Party of China points out:

> The right of ownership by the people's communes, production brigades and production teams and their power of decision must be protected effectively by the laws of the state; it is not permitted to commandeer the manpower, funds products and material by any production team.

This stipulation protects the peasants' collective ownership system and respects the socialist initiative of the peasantry.

The question has been raised as to whether there is a limit to respecting the production team's rights to decide its own affairs. In essence, this question concerns the relationship between state planning and the production teams' rights of decision. This matter should not cause any problems. China is a socialist country, and one of the features of a socialist economy is the exercise of planning on the basis of public ownership. In addition to planning by the state, there is also the right of decision on the part of the grassroots collective economies. The two should be closely integrated, with the planned economy in the lead, supplemented by market regulation.

There are many successful instances of such integration. There should be no attempt to negate the production team's right of decision simply because China has a planned economy, and vice versa. Both tendencies would be incorrect, and both are easily avoided in actual work.

In order to carry through the policy of respecting the production team's rights of decision, an important change is taking place in the people's commune system; economic management in the communes will gradually be separated from government administration. Though it is necessary to handle this matter with caution, the trend is inevitable.

4. Readjusting the Structure of Production and Developing a Diversified Economy

Readjusting the structure of production and developing a diversified economy is a major policy in China's agricultural economy. In the past, there was a tendency toward one-sided emphasis on crop cultivation in the agricultural economy, and on grain production in crop cultivation. Actually, China's agricultural economy displayed a good deal of variety in its original state. In the broad sense, agriculture includes farming, forestry, animal husbandry, sideline occupations and fishery; and even in a more narrow sense, it comprises cereals, cash crops, medicinal crops, fruit trees, and vegetables. Why, then, in some people's thinking, was grain stressed to the exclusion of all other crops? The reason lies in the size of China's population, the backwardness of her agricultural forces of production, and low productivity in agriculture. The people's first concern was to solve the problem of having enough grain to eat. The ancient Chinese aphorism, "grain keeps the people happy", was a reflection of the poorly developed productive forces in the people's economic thinking.

At present, maintaining sufficient supplies of grain is still a most pressing economic problem in the relatively backward nations of the third world. It is not without reason that the international community has made "eliminating the fear of want" one of its broad objectives. People with an ultra-"Leftist" viewpoint, however, exaggerated this point and maintained that since the peoples of the third world had not yet solved their food problems, there could be no fundamental guarantee for the solution of the food problem of China. They believed that the absolute objective of the agricultural economy should be to solve the food problem, with all agricultural resources being directed toward that end.

This one-sided emphasis on grain seriously hampered the development of a diversified economy. And during the "cultural revolution" such one-sidedness was blown up to ridiculous proportions. Making grain the sole crop was regarded as "revolutionary"; planting any other crops was heretical and subject to public censure. As a result, due to various historical reasons, serious imbalances appeared in the structure of agricultural production. First, the proportion crop cultivation took up in the agricultural economy was too large, while that of forestry, animal husbandry, sideline occupations and fishery was too small. In 1978, the output value of crop cultivation was 67.8 percent of the gross national value of agricultural output. Second, in crop cultivation itself, the proportion of grain crops was too high while that of cash crops was too low. The total output value of grain crops made up roughly 70 percent of the total output value of all crops, while that of cash crops and other crops accounted for only about 30 percent.

In order to rectify these disproportions in agriculture, the Party and government made a major decision — they called on agricultural departments throughout the country to carry out readjustment of the agricultural sector and diversification of the agricultural economy. The communique of the Third Plenary Session pointed out that the principle of developing farming, forestry, animal husbandry, sideline production and fishery simultaneously should be implemented. Subsequently, the Fourth Plenary Session passed the "Decisions of the Central Committee of the Communist Party of China on Some Questions Concerning the Acceleration of Agricultural Development", which stated that:

> . . . placing a strong emphasis on grain production was correct, though underemphasizing and causing the deterioration of cash crops, forestry, animal husbandry, and fishery, as well as failing to maintain an ecological balance, taught us an important lesson. We must make optimum use of China's superior natural conditions and tap latent potential in all areas of endeavor in order to bring about large-scale developments in agriculture, forestry and animal husbandry. . . . In a planned way, we must bring about changes in the present structure of agricultural crops and the people's diet, and reform the present situation wherein an emphasis is placed on planting grain and insufficient importance is given to planting economic crops, forestry, animal husbandry, sideline production and fishery.

Satisfactory results were achieved by these efforts: in spite of a reduction of the total area sown with grain in 1979, higher yields per unit of land raised the gross output by 5.2 percent, or 16.54 million tons; the area given over to oil crops was increased, and gross output rose by 24.35 million tons, or 23.3 percent; increases were also registered in cotton, sugar crops, fiber crops, silkworm cocoons and tea leaves; the total output value from crop cultivation increased by 7,108 million yuan over the previous year. In forestry, the total area of afforested land increased, and output value from forestry rose by

1.3 percent over the preceding year. An overall increase was also registered in animal husbandry, with the production of pork, beef and mutton increasing by more than 2.4 million tons, or 24.1 percent. The output value from animal husbandry rose by 2,822 million yuan, or 14.6 percent over the previous year. In fact, heartening progress was observed in all aspects of agriculture — farming, forestry, animal husbandry, sideline production and fishery.

In sum, two major changes took place in the agricultural economy since the readjustments in production. First, without affecting the overall rise in agricultural production, more cash crops (particularly rape) were planted, thus increasing the peasants' incomes. Secondly, while output from crop cultivation continued to increase, animal husbandry registered fairly large advances, so that per capita meat consumption also increased.

Further readjustments were made in agriculture in 1982. Statistics show that in 1982, the gross output value from agriculture, calculated in terms of 1980 prices, was 262,900 million yuan, or 20 percent more than in 1979. Further changes took place in the overall output value of agriculture as a whole, with the proportion of crop cultivation decreasing somewhat and that of forestry, animal husbandry, sidelines and fishery increasing.

Table 15

OUTPUT VALUE OF CROP AND NON-CROP PRODUCTION
IN 1979 AND 1982

(Percentage)

	1979	1982	increase/decrease
Crop cultivation	66.9	62.7	− 4.2
Forestry	2.8	4.1	+ 1.3
Husbandry	14.0	15.5	+ 1.5
Sidelines	15.1	16.0	+ 0.9
Fishery	1.2	1.7	+ 0.5

Meanwhile, a new tendency toward specialization in production was creating an extremely favorable situation in agriculture.

The ratios among the various branches of crop cultivation, particularly that of grain to cash crops, continued to change in a favorable direction. Land planted with grain decreased, but the "lost" land had been unsuited to grain cultivation in the first place, and such readjustments were basically rectifications of past mistakes. The situation regarding this land was quite complex. Some of it was more suited to planting rape, and grain planted on it in the first year grew poorly. On other areas of land grain crops were not necessarily poor, but planting grain on them did not pay, with the result that the peasants' incomes from the land had decreased.

There were different reasons for the increase in the area sown with cash crops. Some land was switched from grain to cash crops because it was better suited to the latter. Other areas were too saline or alkaline for grain crops to grow well, so the peasants planted sunflowers or beets since they stood to lose very little from doing so. On other plots crops were changed according to unified plans which brought cropping systems in line with local conditions. In 1980, for example, after conducting studies on the demarcation of agricultural regions, Zunhua County in Hebei Province readjusted its crop layout and cropping system, reducing the area given over to two-harvest-per-year crops and increasing that of crops producing three harvests every two years, while making efforts to develop forestry and animal husbandry. As a result, the grain crop that year increased by 65.15 million *jin*, breaking all previous records. Meanwhile, the peanut crop increased by 55.3 percent, the number of sheep and goats by 6.6 percent, gross income by 5 percent and the commune members' income from collective distribution by 13.4 percent.*

The State Council and related departments also adopted a series of policies and measures to further diversify the economy

---

* From *Rural Work Newsletter*, May 1981 issue

and improve the agricultural sector. Among the more important of these was the policy of setting up links between regions of concentrated sugar and cotton production with grain growing regions, and increasing grain imports so as to step up the development of cash crops in order to end cotton and sugar imports within three to five years; the policy of giving special assistance to farming areas designated as commodity grain bases and using their increased output to help other regions readjust their choices of crops; and the policy of stabilizing state purchases of grain and reducing or canceling such purchases in regions afflicted by economic difficulties. As regards forestry, most regions have given greater attention not only to planting trees but also to the survival rate. The northern provinces have continued to step up construction of shelter belt systems. In plain areas, vigorous afforestation drives have resulted in huge increases in the total afforested area. In these regions, the main thrust is toward constructing "farmland forest networks", i.e., surrounding each piece of farmland with trees so that, from the air, they resemble a green checkerboard. This significant new development has the advantage of conserving soil, moisture and fertilizer and improving the microclimate.

With respect to animal husbandry, the former one-sided emphasis on increasing the year-end number of livestock "in the pen" has been replaced by new stresses on raising the ratio of animals ready for slaughter, the amount of meat produced by each animal and the percentage of marketed animals. At the same time, efforts have been made to raise more herbivorous animals; this is a matter of special significance in China where there is hardly enough farmland and grain for the large population. The rural areas are still the main source of pork, and to maintain a steady supply an emphasis is placed on stabilizing hog raising policies and implementing the principle of raising hogs mainly by private households.

With regard to rural industries and sideline production, continued emphasis is being placed on brigade-run industries and on experiments with agricultural-industrial-commercial combines. Attention is also being paid to traditional sidelines and the manufacture of native and special local products. More than a thousand sites for the production of local products have been set up nationwide. The several dozen traditional products they turn out comprise 60 percent of the state purchases of such products.

In fishery, reforms of strategic significance have been instituted. In all regions, the emphasis has shifted from catching to raising fish in order to protect China's aquatic resources and ensure that fishery production maintains a constant rate of increase. In ocean fishery, restrictions have been placed on offshore fishing and pelagic fishing is being developed. Meanwhile, policies on fishery have been relaxed to encourage aquiculture by rural communes and brigades.

The above-mentioned measures have done much to effect more rational proportions in agriculture, make better use of natural resources and develop a multi-sided rural economy. But much more remains to be done in this field.

(1)   Enormous economic benefits can be gained from using the abundant resources found in the mountainous areas, which make up about two-thirds of China's territory. But the economies in the mountainous regions are at present making very slow progress. One of the many reasons for this state of affairs is the difficulty of transport. Efforts must be made to improve communications in the mountainous regions and perfect the purchasing and marketing system so that mountain produce, now ignored for lack of transport, will find its way into the market. This will also help to develop the local economies.

(2)   There is a great potential to be tapped in the pastoral areas, but first more work must be done on grassland construction, and scientific grazing must be instituted. China has four billion *mu* of grasslands, a billion *mu* of grass-covered hills and slopes, and another billion more *mu* of land producing stalks and chaff suitable for fodder. These provide conditions for large-scale development of animal husbandry.

(3)   Much can also be done in the area of aquiculture. Of the fresh and salt water areas suitable for this purpose, only 55 percent of the former and 23.6 percent of the latter are being

used at present. And output from aquiculture is low due to poor management. There is a large potential for raising fish in ponds, but the national average output of fish per *mu* of pond surface is only 96 *jin*, whereas some of the more productive brigades and teams produce as much as two or three thousand *jin* per *mu*. Output of fish could be raised several fold by good management.

A more far-reaching aspect of readjusting the agricultural sector and developing a many-sided economy is that these trends will help to balance the ecology and create conditions for further growth in agriculture. Zhenba County in Shaanxi Province once had a forest cover rate of 60 percent, and floods, droughts and hail were rare. Later, however, many trees were cut down to clear the land for farming when the county started to place a one-sided emphasis on grain production. Production of timber and forestry sidelines dropped and, what was worse, floods, droughts and hailstorms increased and the soil became seriously eroded. Once a rainstorm destroyed more than 30,000 *mu* of paddy fields. Grain output fell, and only began to rise again after the county authorities rectified their mistakes and made efforts to restore the ecological balance by developing a multi-sided economy.

Another important point is that restructuring agriculture and developing sidelines provides reliable outlets for surplus rural labor. A conspicuous disadvantage in China's rural economy is the overall shortage of land and the small amount of farmland per capita. There is, however, the advantage of an abundance of resources. Proper use of these resources by means of large-scale development of agricultural sidelines will provide work for much surplus labor. Of particular significance is the fact that since farming is a highly seasonal occupation, a multi-sided agricultural economy will permit the simultaneous running of undertakings wherein work time can be staggered. This will give peasants more opportunities to develop and use their talents. Readjusting the structure of agriculture and developing sidelines is thus not only of current significance, but has an important bearing on the long-term development of Chinese agriculture.

5.   Relaxing Restrictions to Develop Household Sidelines

Among the policies and measures adopted for the agricultural economy after the Third Plenum of the Party, one of those most welcome by the peasants was that of relaxing restrictions on individual management to encourage household sidelines.

Individual management refers to commune members engaging in some form of agricultural production apart from their productive activities in the collective. This may take the form of working a private plot of land (a private herd in pastoral areas, or a private grove of trees in a forestry region) or engaging in some household sideline or raising chickens, ducks, bees or rabbits. The policy permitting peasants to engage in such individual management was defined during the period of the agricultural producers' cooperatives, but was never properly implemented because of the "Leftist" thinking that came into fashion. The main points of the policy are as follows:

1. Peasants are permitted and encouraged to farm private plots of land.

Given the actual state of China's rural economy, there are many advantages to be derived from this. First, this helps to satisfy some of the peasants' everyday needs by providing vegetables, miscellaneous grains and other farm produce. Such a variety would not be possible if sole reliance were placed on what the collective economy can supply. Secondly, private plots can be planted with grain where such crops are in short supply. In some places, the peasants grow sweet potatoes.* The stems are fed to the peasants' pigs, thus solving at once the problem of pig fodder as well as food for human consumption. And lastly, produce from private plots, sold on the market, provides the peasants with cash.

Do the peasants' private plots constitute capitalism? People with ultra-"Leftist" thinking brand all forms of economy out-

---

* Potatoes and sweet potatoes are regarded as grain crops in China.

side of the collective economy as capitalist. This is ridiculous. Private plots in China's socialistic cooperatives are no more than a minor supplement and adjunct to the socialist collective economy and have nothing to do with capitalist economy. They are one of the "small freedoms in the big collective". In 1981, the government made an important amendment to its policies in line with the actual state of development of the rural economy: "In places where production is not contracted to the individual households, the area of private plots and fodder plots may be increased in the light of local conditions. The amount of land for these two purposes may comprise a maximum of 15 percent of the total area of farmland in the production brigades." Statistics show that the commune members' private plots in the Chinese countryside in 1978 amounted to 85.58 million *mu*, or 5.7 percent of the total area of farmland in that year. By 1981, the area had increased 39.6 percent to 33.86 million *mu*, or 8 percent of the total area of farmland in that year.

In implementing the policy on private plots, the following regulations were drawn up: (1) As with commune members who cultivate private plots distributed by the collective, peasants in pastoral and mountainous regions may similarly retain a small number of private livestock. All private plots and private livestock are protected by state law, and no organization or individual may interfere in this matter. (2) The cultivation of the private plots must be organized by the commune members themselves, and all private plots forcibly confiscated in the past must be returned to the commune members. (3) The nature and quantity of what is planted in the private plots is to be decided by the commune members themselves, and no organization or individual may arbitrarily decree what they are to plant or not to plant. (4) The produce from private plots belongs to the commune members who plant them, and no organization or individual may "transfer" it to themselves under any pretext or in any form. Commune members have the right to dispose of their own produce; they may consume it themselves or sell it on the market. (5) The size of private plots is determined by unified state policy and local regulations, and cannot be expanded without authorization. If large discrepancies arise in the size of private plots due to such factors as population shifts, with permission from the county authorities adjustments may be made according to the present number of inhabitants within the production brigade or team, on condition that the total area of private plots remains unchanged.

2. The commune members are encouraged to develop household sidelines. Because of the meager economic foundations in the Chinese countryside, it is not yet possible to ensure that peasant households will become well-off by relying solely on the collective economy. A 1979 survey shows that 27.3 percent of all production teams in China had annual per capita incomes from collective distribution of less than 50 yuan. In these production teams, the commune members had a hard time keeping themselves fed and clothed, not to mention becoming well-off. In order to change this state of affairs it was necessary to emphasize the development of household sidelines in addition to improving and consolidating the collective economy.

There are many types of sidelines which peasant households can engage in. They may raise pigs, sheep, goats, poultry, bees and silkworms; cultivate vegetables, melons and fruit trees as well as bamboo and trees for timber; or manufacture woven goods and handicrafts. These sidelines are usually engaged in during slack farming seasons or all year round by "auxiliary labor power",* but with the development of such sidelines, households specializing in or engaged mainly in such occupations have appeared. Animal husbandry is perhaps the most popular sideline. Incomplete statistics compiled at a meeting on animal husbandry in northern China held in August 1982 revealed that throughout China some 560,000 households were specializing in this occupation and another 1.77 million households engaged mainly in this occupation. These households had a total of more than 10 million large animals,** 58 million

---

* Members of the household other than the main breadwinners.
** Large animals — cattle, horses, mules, donkeys and camels.

chickens, 12 million rabbits and 570,000 swarms of bees. Calculated according to the fixed prices in 1970, the value of output from household sidelines in 1981 was 34,980 million yuan, or 20.3 percent of the total agricultural output in that year. That is to say, one-fifth of the farm and sideline production in China was turned out by household sidelines.

In 1981, the government passed an important regulation to encourage commune members to develop household sidelines. The regulation stipulates that "the initiative of both the collective and the individual should be brought into play", and that the production brigades should "actively encourage and support the commune members in engaging in service trades, handicrafts, animal raising and transport and marketing businesses either individually or in partnership, and all items suited to management by individual commune members should as much as possible be operated by the peasant households themselves with organization and assistance from the production brigades". The regulation also decrees that "in times other than busy farming seasons, commune members who fall into the category of semi-labor power and auxiliary labor power should be allowed to refrain from participation in collective labor and devote their whole attention to whatever household sidelines they are capable of engaging in".

3.   Expanding country fairs. The commodity circulation structure of China's national economy consists in the main of two sections: state-run commerce and cooperative commerce. Another important channel, supplementing these two, is the market fairs in the countryside.   This form of commerce is protected by state policy. All country fairs closed down during the "cultural revolution" have been revived beginning in 1978.

The necessity of maintaining such a policy is underscored by the fact that China's socialist economy is still a commodity economy.   Thus not only should commodity production be permitted and encouraged, conditions should be created for the exchange and circulation of commodities as well.   Since the peasants are allowed to cultivate small private plots and encouraged to develop household sidelines, there is a need for a corresponding development of market fair trade. Moreover, as household sidelines turn out products in small and scattered lots which are difficult for state and cooperative commerce to handle in a unified manner, market fairs make up for the latter's deficiencies in this respect. By August 1982, there were more than 43,000 market fairs in the Chinese countryside and about 3,000 urban markets for farm and sideline produce. Transactions in the rural market fairs rose from 17,000 million yuan in 1979 to over 20,000 million yuan in 1981.

Rural market fair commerce is conducted under the auspices and control of the government, and is a necessary supplement to state and cooperative commerce. But since it differs in essence from commercial institutions, market fair commerce should be strictly controlled and guided. In the past, the controls instituted were usually too rigid, and when the controls were relaxed, the result was confusion. Well-run market fairs can liven up commodity circulation, promote the rural economy and bring greater variety into peasants' lives.

6. Carrying Out the Policy of Payment According to Work Done

The principle of a worker obtaining compensation in proportion to the quantity and quality of the labor he or she provides is known as "to each according to his work". "From each according to his ability, to each according to his work" is the principle of distribution practiced under socialism, and applies to industry and farms under state ownership as well as to agriculture where the main form of ownership is collective.

Ever since the cooperative movement began, China has regarded the principle of "to each according to his work" as a basic policy in collectively run agriculture. The communist principle of "from each according to his ability, to each according to his needs" is not yet realizable because society cannot yet provide the abundance of products necessary for this advanced form of distribution. Thus China must go through a transitional period during which the creation of a set of measures which conform to transitional principles and policies must be actively encouraged. China's policy of "to each according to his work" is based on the direct contribution of each worker to society. This differs from the capitalist distribution system whereby the worker contributes indirectly to society by selling his labor to the capitalist, who serves as an intermediary between labor and the means of production.

Although "to each according to his work" has consistently been the policy for China's collective economy, it was carried out poorly for a long period of time. The reasons were both social and economic. This omission not only afflicted the peasants' thinking and lives; it cast a shadow on the entire agricultural economy. In 1978, the Third Plenum of the Party's Eleventh Central Committee solved this problem, and the policy is now again being implemented widely.

Social factors were the greatest obstacle to the implementation of this policy. The Chinese have an ancient saying, "Poverty is better than inequality." The ideological background to this saying is clearly some concept of "social equity", which itself originated in the world outlook of the small producer when social production was at a low level of development. The broad social basis of the concept is shown by the fact that Chinese history abounds with legendary heroes and peasant insurgents who plundered the rich to aid the poor. This concept, however, is completely at odds with the world outlook of scientific proletarians who observe and analyze social and historical phenomena and the objective world dialectically, as well as from the point of view of the development of the social forces of production. Their belief that scientific socialism will continue to grow while capitalism withers away is not based on mere concepts, but on the fact that the socialist system is better suited to the needs of developing the social forces of production. In China, however, the concept of "social equity" with its long traditions and far-reaching influence will not be easily eradicated. Its influence is felt in an impalpable yet persistent way through a form of social thinking that is constantly infiltrating the socialist system. The most systematic and concentrated form of expression it takes is egalitarianism.

Another and perhaps more fundamental reason for the difficulty of implementing the system of payment according to work is China's poor economic foundation, low level of production and enormous population. National income per capita is very low, particularly in agriculture. The following table shows the differences in the amount of national income created by the agricultural and non-agricultural sectors in China over the years.

Table 16

PER CAPITA AGRICULTURAL AND NON-AGRICULTURAL INCOME, 1949-1979

(Unit: yuan/person)

Year	Population as a whole (average)	Agricultural population (average)	Non-agricultural population (average)
1949	66	55	120
1952	102	69	300
1957	140	79	455
1962	137	79	426
1965	191	106	615
1970	233	113	926
1975	272	126	1,098
1977	281	123	1,176
1978	314	132	1,312
1979	347	161	1,310

This table shows that the average cash income of the agricultural population in 1977, 1978 and 1979 was only 43.8, 42.0 and 46.4 percent of that of the population as a whole; and only 10.5, 10.1 and 12.3 percent of that of the non-agricultural population. The low average income of the agricultural population was an important factor for the prevalence of egalitarianism in the agricultural sector.

In pursuing their ultra-"Leftist" line, Lin Biao and the Gang of Four played up egalitarian thinking in society by criticizing peasants' rights to earn profits and workpoints. Instead, a system of "political workpoints" was instituted by which payment for labor was calculated according to political attitude. This practice was at complete variance with the principle of "to each according to his work". It created considerable confusion and engendered unhealthy tendencies in the agricultural economy. The Regulations for the Rural People's Communes (Draft for Trial Implementation) explicitly stipulated:

> All levels of economic organizations within the people's communes must conscientiously carry out the principles of "from each according to his ability, to each according to his work, more payment for more work, and equal payment for men and women performing the same work", improve management of the quota system, offer remuneration according to the amount and quality of work performed, establish a rational system of rewards and punishments, and take appropriate measures to correct egalitarianism.

Marked results have been obtained since these regulations were put into effect. Wherever they have been conscientiously implemented, and wherever the principle of "more payment for more work" has been adhered to, the masses' enthusiasm is high and farm and sideline production has registered swift and healthy advances.

The system of "to each according to his work" as practiced by the production brigades consists in dividing, according to the work done by each individual, the farm and sideline products and/or income created by brigade members in the course of collective production, after deducting taxes, production expenses, depreciation charges and management expenses, and after withholding public accumulation and welfare funds. This policy is reinforced by the principle of depriving able-bodied workers who do not work of the right to participate in such distribution. To better implement the policy of "to each according to his work", the authorities in all localities are publicizing the benefits of this policy. Earnest efforts are being made to make people see that differences should be allowed to exist and to modify the system of distribution so as to do away with "eating from the common pot".

7. Production Responsibility — A Major Transformation in the Agricultural Management System

The core of the economic policies carried out in the rural areas since the Third Plenum of the Eleventh Central Committee of the Communist Party is the promotion of different forms of production responsibility. Major changes have since taken place in the system of agricultural management in the countryside. The system of linking payment to production which appeared in the course of these developments has, in particular, met with enthusiastic approval from the broad masses of peasants.

To understand why the institution of production responsibility — actually no more than a change in the system and method of management — has had such powerful repercussions in the countryside, one must compare the situation there before and after the system came into being.

Back in the days of the agricultural producers' cooperatives, an initial form of production responsibility had already taken shape in agricultural management. The cooperatives were relatively small in those days — roughly equivalent in size to today's production brigades, and served as the basic unit of accounting in the commune. To facilitate production and labor management, the cooperatives were subdivided into several production teams. The cooperative's manpower, land, draft animals and other means of production came under the jurisdiction of the team, and the management of production and labor was the team's responsibility. But accounting was done by the cooperative, which contracted with the production teams for labor, production and costs, and rewarded the teams if they turned out more products than contracted for. Such was the system practiced in the 1950s. Under this system, the production teams had clearcut responsibilities and differences between teams resulted from the quality of management in each team. Such differences ultimately manifested themselves in distribution as inequalities and disequilibriums among various production teams. This, to a degree, had the effect of according more remuneration to those who worked more, which conforms to the socialist principle of distribution. Furthermore, the competition which actually took place among the various teams spurred the masses' initiative in production and pushed farm and sideline production to higher levels. This system was later taken over by the production teams under the people's communes. In retrospect, it is evident that this form of management did, to a certain extent, give expression to socialist principles and brought into play the advantages of socialist agriculture. But it failed to provide a fundamental solution to the problem of "eating from the common pot".

After the outbreak of the "cultural revolution" in 1966, the system of contracts and rewards mentioned above was criticized as revisionist and abolished. Thereafter, all administrative systems in the agricultural economy were discarded, management became lax, the initiative of the production teams sank, and even "eating from the common pot" was no longer possible. Agricultural production reached a low ebb. Moreover, in many localities, the people's communes took to issuing arbitrary and impracticable orders which only worsened the peasants' plight.

As political life in the countryside became more democratic after the fall of the Gang of Four, production management systems were gradually restored and the agricultural economy came to life again. In these circumstances, the Central Committee of the Communist Party in 1979 promulgated a document entitled "On a Number of Problems Concerning the Further Strengthening and Perfection of the Responsibility System in Agriculture", which emphasized that different forms of management should be allowed to coexist in the light of local conditions. This document was naturally welcome by the peasantry, and within a short time, about 99 percent of the approximately six million basic accounting units in China established various forms of job responsibility.

Experience has shown that this major transformation in the rural management system is of such far-reaching significance and has such a profound impact on the peasants' interests that its social and economic importance is only rivaled by the land reform and the movement for agricultural collectivization. In the course of this transformation, people are once more taking stock of many well-known traditional concepts, such as the relations between collective and personal creativity, the social nature of labor, the role of the individual in the collective, the links between the household and society, and the ethical and economic value of the household. And with the development and perfection of the system of production responsibility, new economic and social relationships are being formed — links that are essentially based on the social value of labor. This will put an end once and for all to the practice of "eating from the common pot", drive away the specter of egalitarianism and establish an appropriate balance between personal responsibility and social welfare.

The systems of responsibility for agricultural production now being adopted in the rural areas fall, by and large, into two categories. One is the "work-contract responsibility system" which is not linked to output, and the other is the "output-contract responsibility system".

Under the work-contract responsibility system a work group or household contracts with the production team to perform a certain job in a certain number of days. Once the job is done, workpoints are accorded according to the contract. In general, this system involves contracts for specialized work, such as that involving animal husbandry, field crops or fertilizer. The advantage of this system is that it makes use of skilled labor and raises work efficiency. In some places work is contracted out to specialized households or individuals as well as to work groups. Sometimes the work is contracted out by levels: The work group contracts for work from the production team, and then subcontracts it out to households and individuals. Under this system, the responsibilities are set forth clearly and standards are stipulated for giving rewards or imposing sanctions. The implementation of the work-contract responsibility system has aided in the elimination of shoddy, haphazard work and egalitarian distribution.

Another form of this system is the short-term work contract, best suited to work groups of a temporary or seasonal nature. The production brigade contracts short-term jobs to the work groups or to households and individuals, stipulating the quantity and quality of the work, the responsibility of each person and the number of workpoints involved. In these respects the work-contract system surpasses the responsibility system practiced during the time of the cooperatives.

The output-contract responsibility system evolved out of the work-contract system, but once it was implemented it immediately manifested unexpected vitality. Under this system, the production team is divided into a number of work groups which contract for both specific plots of land and types of work and for the output therefrom. The production team need not concern itself with the amount of manpower and investment required to complete the assignment; all it has to do is to inspect and accept the products after a job is done. By now the output-contract system accounts for more than 90 percent of the various responsibility systems practiced in the rural areas.

The output-contract system also exists in many different forms, the most common being the system known as "contracting by specializations with payment linked to output". The production team divides its farm work into a number of specializations which are contracted out to specialized groups. The output achieved under such an arrangement is distributed by the production team, which dispenses rewards to groups which exceed their contract quotas and imposes fines on those which produce less. This system of responsibility is generally suited to work which calls for a fair degree of skill. The contracting unit may be a household or individual with special skills, or a work team.

Experience shows that there is a great future in the rural areas for this last type of responsibility system. For one thing, it is based on a division of labor according to specializations. Secondly, the responsibilities under this system are clearly defined, as are the rewards and penalties. Production Team No. 8 of the Aotou Brigade in Xing'an Commune, Guangxi, was one of the poorest teams in the commune. After the implementation of the system of linking payment to output in early 1979, marked changes occurred within one year. Total grain production showed an increase of 40 percent over that of the previous year, and average per capita income increased by more than 60 percent.

The implementation of the system of "contracting by specializations and linking payment to output" has inevitably given rise to fairly large differentials in the incomes of peasant households and individuals. This is mainly a consequence of varying levels of technical skills and management. However, since these differences in incomes arise from differences in the amount of labor expended rather than from the exploitation of other people's labor, they should be permitted and even encouraged. For such differences will benefit production in general by spurring the peasants to acquire scientific knowledge and technical skills.

Changes have also taken place in the management and administration of production teams ever since the system of contracting by specializations was implemented. Division of labor has become more rational. A division of labor based on mutual reliance has taken shape among the specialized groups, households and individuals, and the labor efficiency of each has risen, with the result that the economic returns of the team as a whole have also increased.

Another form of the responsibility system is based on linking payment with output without division by specializations. This is generally called "contracting output to work groups". While continuing to practice unified planning, management and accounting, the production team contracts farmwork to be done on a certain amount of land to be work teams. The contract fixes the amount of personnel, land, workpoints and output, as well as the cost of production. Produce within the amount specified in the contract is handed over to the production team for unified distribution; that which exceeds the specified amount is disposed of by the contracting work groups. Within the work team itself the original system of assigning workpoints according to work quotas is retained. Fears have been expressed that this responsibility system may in fact break the production team down into small units. This may appear to be the case, especially since the personnel and land are fixed by contract. But in fact it is not so, because the production team retains the powers of unified planning management, administration, finances and distribution. This, plus the fact that the land is still owned by the collective, ensures that this kind of responsibility system will neither fragment the production teams nor become a starting point for the restoration of the old order.

Perhaps the most striking economic change brought about by the institution of the responsibility system in agriculture is the appearance of the "output-contract with the household". With the "output-contract with the household", the contracting household undertakes to achieve a specified output, for which it receives a stipulated number of workpoints; rewards are given for excess output. Under the "output-contract with the household" system, the household may keep whatever output remains after paying an agricultural tax, selling a specified amount of output to the state, and contributing a certain sum to the collective's public accumulation and public welfare funds. Because of its simplicity and straightforwardness, this system is favored by the peasants in many localities. A feature of the system is the placing of responsibility for production on the peasant household economy, and the expansion of the household's role in agricultural production through closely linking farm work with sideline production.

The widespread development of the "output-contract with the household" in China's rural economy has drawn considerable attention in economic circles at home and abroad. If we trace it back to its roots, however, it will be seen that this form of responsibility was being utilized in some localities in the 1960s.

The now-legendary story begins in 1960* when China was struggling with the difficulties engendered by the "Great Leap Forward" and a series of severe natural calamities. A 70-year-old peasant in Anhui Province, whose son had contracted tuberculosis and was unable to work or support his father, was advised by his people's commune to enter a home for the aged. Unwilling to live at public expense, the old man requested his production team to allow him to take his ailing son up into the mountains where he could care for him and at the same time farm some wasteland. The old man offered to give the state any excess grain he grew on the land; and in case the grain proved insufficient for his needs, he promised not to apply to the state for relief. The commune agreed to his request.

In the mountains, the old man put 16 *mu* of wasteland under cultivation and harvested 1,650 kilograms of grain the first year. From this he deducted 750 kilograms for food, seed and fodder, and turned the rest over to the commune. He also earned a substantial amount from raising pigs and chickens. The old man suggested to the commune leadership that all the commune's land should be contracted out to the commune's members if the collective economy was to prosper, since this would stimulate the peasants' sense of responsibility. The income, he said, could be distributed by the collective. This proposal came to the notice of the provincial leadership, which canvassed a large number of peasants on the matter. When the peasants expressed their approval, the new form of responsibility was promoted throughout the province under the name "fixing output for each piece of land and responsibility for each person", later abbreviated to "responsibility fields" or "output-contract with the household". This form of production arrangement evolved mostly into "overall contracts with the house-

---

* Quoted from Yang Xunwen's "Output Contracting with the Household Is an Important Matter of Theory and Policy", *Selected Articles on the Agricultural Economy*, March 1980, p. 50.

hold", which produced excellent results not only in Anhui but in other provinces as well.

But this new form of responsibility was repeatedly attacked by the "Left". In 1962, when the countryside was just beginning to recover from its economic difficulties, the "output-contract with the household" was subjected to attack from many sides and criticized as an attempt to "divide up the land and go it alone" and to "restore capitalism". In Anhui Province, where 85.4 percent of the production teams were practicing the new system, orders were given in 1962 to "rectify" the situation at once. By 1963 agriculture had reverted to a state where no individual households took responsibility for production. And after the "cultural revolution" began in 1966, further criticism was leveled at the "output-contract with the household". It came into its own again only after the downfall of the Gang of Four.

Those who oppose the "output-contract with the household" equate it with "dividing up the land and going it alone" on the grounds that, firstly, labor under such an arrangement is no longer collective but "conducted by individual household", and, secondly, that differences in income among contracting households will lead to "class differentiation". Actually, neither of these arguments are tenable. The socialist nature of the collective economy is not determined by a specific form of joint labor. In the collective economy, workers engage in joint labor in the sense that labor under the socialist system is directly social in nature and that public ownership of the means of production makes it necessary and possible to organize labor in a planned way on a society-wide basis. Thus the labor of each worker inevitably forms part of the joint labor of society as a whole, irrespective of the nature or location of the work. It is both ridiculous and impracticable to define social labor as labor where many laborers work together on the same work site. Due to the enormous rise in labor productivity in modern industry, entire workshops are often operated by a single worker, a tendency which is bound to become more widespread as modernization progresses. There is no reason to conclude that increases in labor productivity will cause social labor to retrogress from collective joint labor to "going it alone".

Although the "output-contract with the household" devolves production and management to the individual household, it is presupposed that the production team exercises unified leadership and planning and that the land remains under public ownership. Hence, the "output-contract with the household" exists only in the sense of being a form of responsibility for production. There are no grounds for equating it with "dividing up the land and going it alone".

Furthermore, there is nothing reproachable about the fact that the "output-contract with the household" leads to differences in income among peasant households. Before the responsibility system was implemented in the countryside, the income distributed in the production team was often very much the same for each of its members, so that those who worked better and harder received no rewards and those who worked less well did not learn the lesson they deserved. The result was shoddy, irresponsible work detrimental to the development of farm and sideline production. Therein lies the necessity and advantages of the system of responsibility for production. The fact that a number of peasant households which work well and practice good management will become prosperous before other households accords with the laws of development of the agricultural economy and, furthermore, will help to spur more peasants onto the path of prosperity. Moreover, as the material wellbeing of those who achieve early prosperity is based on their own labor and not on exploitation of others, there is no question of "class polarization". It is utterly wrong to lump class polarization based on exploitation together with differences in income resulting from good or bad work.

While the "output-contract with the household" functions under state ownership within a unified collective economy, it is true that they narrow the scope of management down to the household. This, however, is an objective necessity dictated by economic laws.

We know that any viable production system must rest upon

a suitable socio-economic basis. The economic basis cannot be divorced from the forces of production. China's collective-ownership economy was set up before the productive forces had achieved any considerable state of development and still remains at the "handicraft workshop" stage. Any realistic appraisal of China's agricultural forces of production will show that they are still at a very low level, and have not yet reached a high degree of socialization. The rural economy remains in a state of self-sufficiency or semi-self-sufficiency, and the merchandising of its products is as yet partial and incomplete. These are the factors that determine the relations of production in China's rural economy and dictate the fact the "output-contract" should limit the scope of management to the household. People cannot choose their production relations, no more than they can decide the level of their forces of production. Such is the social and economic basis for the widespread development of the "output-contract with the household" in China's rural economy today.

Another reason for the popularity of the "output-contract with the household" is that it is a reaction to the "Leftist" ways of doing things prevalent for many years. In those years the size of the collective economic unit and the degree of public ownership was often emphasized without regard for objective conditions, and so-called "communist" transfers of land and property were effected in order to artificially enlarge the economic units and raise the degree of public ownership. These "Leftist" mistakes seriously damaged the peasants' economic interests and took away much or all of their enthusiasm for collective labor. Allowing the peasants to engage in contract production is actually a step backward to prepare for fresh advances. When the conditions are ripe, the peasants will voluntarily form associations again on a new basis.

The vitality of the output-contract system is shown by concrete advances in farm and sideline production. In the past, the peasants in the Heze district of Shandong Province had to buy grain nearly every year from the government — more than 2.5 million *jin* between 1955 and 1967 — and received state relief and free financial investments. The introduction of the output-contract system has brought about big increase in production: in 1980, the local peasants sold 350 million *jin* of grain, 18 million *jin* of peanuts and 1.24 million *dan* of cotton to the state. The Chuxian region, in Anhui Province, was long known as a poverty-stricken district. But after the popularization of the output-contract system there in 1980, increases were registered in all crops throughout all the counties in the district, in spite of a serious flood that year. A saying among the local peasants goes: "With the contract system, in one year we'll have enough to eat, in two years we'll have spending money, and in three we'll be well off — so long as the policies don't change!"

The emergence of many different forms of production responsibility in agriculture is a very good thing. Circumstances vary considerably in different parts of China, and it is neither desirable nor possible to demand that things be done the same way everywhere. It is imperative to adhere to the principles of taking local conditions into account, proceeding from reality, allowing the masses to decide their own affairs, and encouraging creativity and versatility. There must be no repetition of the mistakes of "eating from the common pot", instituting overly rigid controls, issuing impracticable orders and insisting on uniformity. Efforts must be made to play up the advantages of the collective economy and at the same time mobilize the initiative of the broad masses of peasants in order to raise agricultural production to new heights.

Certain patterns can be discerned in the way the many different forms of production responsibility have been implemented in the rural areas since the Third Plenum of the Party's Eleventh Central Committee. Generally speaking, the system of contracting by specialization with payment linked to output has been adopted in regions with a flourishing economy, a well-developed commodity economy, an abundance of agricultural means of production, a high level of production, a fairly high degree of division of labor, and conditions for practicing unified management. On the other hand, places with poor economic

conditions and underdeveloped productive forces usually tend
to employ the system of contracting output with the household.

8. The Power of Policy

Enormous changes have occurred in China's countryside in
the few years since the new rural economic policies were first
implemented in 1979. The oppressive atmosphere of the years
of the Gang of Four has completely disappeared and has been
replaced by a new dynamism and vitality.

In the winter of 1981, delegates from Shandong to the Fourth
Session of the Fifth National Peoples Congress told reporters
that the average per capita income of commune members in
the province had increased by only 16.48 yuan between 1956
and 1978, or by an average of 0.75 yuan annually. In the last
three years, however, the commune members' incomes had risen
by more than 17 yuan annually. Even more inspiring was the
fact that the once backward Huimin, Dezhou, Liaocheng and
Heze districts were now catching up with the rest of the province. The average per capita income from collective distribution
in these four districts in 1980 increased by 41.40 yuan over that
in 1978, and was expected to rise by another 30 yuan in 1981,
resulting in individual incomes of 120 yuan.

As in all other districts, the economic advance in the four
backward districts mentioned above were brought about by
the new rural policies. A rough count made in 29 provinces,
municipalities and autonomous regions in 1982 shows that
34,021 (or 4.9 percent) of the nearly 700,000 production teams
in China achieved a per capita income of more than 300 yuan,
and in 9,507 of these production teams the per capita income
exceeded 400 yuan. Xinlian Brigade in Jiaxing County, Zhejiang Province, increased production and income by integrating
animal husbandry with farming and by developing silkworm
cultivation; the marketable portion of its agricultural produce
was as high as 51 percent and average per capita income

reached 331 yuan. The Zhucha Island Brigade in Qingdao, Shandong Province, once a poverty-stricken fishing community, combined fishery with aquiculture after the implementation of the new agricultural policies; it bagan to raise kelp, mink, sea cucumbers and abalone, and from its increased income distributed an average of 300 yuan to each brigade member. The Huangxiangtan Brigade in Haiyan County, Qinghai Province, rapidly became prosperous by developing animal husbandry; the average per capita income from distribution in this brigade was 438 yuan.

The number of production brigades in China in which per capita income from collective distribution exceeded 300 yuan continued to grow in 1980 and 1981. Their number reached 5,569 in 1980, an increase of 2.4 fold over 1979; and in 1981 there were 10,945 of them, 96.5 percent more than in 1980. Thus, in two years' time the number of such brigades increased more than 5.7 fold.

A sample survey conducted by the State Statistical Bureau among 18,529 rural households in 568 counties of 28 provinces, municipalities and autonomous regions (excluding Tibet) indicates that the incomes (both from collective distribution and household sidelines) of commune members rose by large margins each year since the Party's Third Plenum. Net per capita income (133.6 yuan in 1978) rose by 26.6 yuan in 1979, 31.1 yuan in 1980, and 32.1 yuan in 1981 to reach 223.4 yuan. In three years it had increased by 89.8 yuan, or 67.2 percent, at a rate unprecedented since the founding of the People's Republic in 1949. The commune members' income from household sidelines rose even faster; the net per capita income from this source was 84.5 yuan in 1981, 1.36 percent higher than in 1978.

The effect of the new policies can also be seen in the state of agricultural production in the country as a whole. In 1981, three years after the implementation of these policies, agricultural production and harvests continued to increase with unabated momentum in spite of serious floods and droughts in many regions of China. Gross value of agricultural output in that year was 5.7 percent higher than in 1980; that of crop cultivation increased by 5.3 percent, of forestry by 4 percent, of animal husbandry and fishery by 6 percent, and of sideline production by 6.8 percent. Such remarkable achievements would not have been possible without the new policies.

Chapter VI

NEW DEVELOPMENTS IN THE RURAL
ECONOMY IN THE 1980S

New agricultural policies adopted since the beginning of the 1980s have given rise to new developments that have both changed the outlook of agricultural production and brought about major reforms in the agricultural administrative structure.

Reforms aimed at eliminating the practice of "eating out of the common pot" and popularizing the contract responsibility system were carried out extensively before 1980. But after 1980, these reforms were no longer simply matters of management; they involved the agricultural system as a whole, and an entirely new model of agricultural administration — a Chinese-style administration — has begun to take shape.

The course of this evolution was as follows: (1) Beginning from setting quotas for households to contracting production tasks to individual households, a form of management consisting mainly of the family contract system gradually takes shape. (2) Extensive implementation of the family contract system gives rise to specialized households. (3) A sector of the agricultural population becomes detached from the land as division of labor develops and production becomes more specialized and socialized. (4) Many new types of combined production appear. (5) The "three-level administration with the production team as the basis" breaks down, and the new forms become the principal trend in rural reform.

What follows is a more detailed account of the five stages described above and an estimate of their social and economic significance.

1. All-Round Contracting — the Family Contract Responsibility System

The production responsibility system in its various forms was implemented under China's rural economic policy. Before long, two forms became dominant: One was the quota responsibility system, which evolved from the job responsibility system; and the other was the family contract system, which evolved from the collective contract system. Since 1980 the family contract system has taken precedence in most of China's rural areas. Meanwhile, a simple form of the responsibility system, called the "all-round contract system", came into being. The most dramatic changes took place between the autumn of 1981 and the autumn of 1982. In this period the majority of the Chinese peasants turned to the system of all-round household contracting.

In 1983, a signed article published by the agricultural authorities in Sichuan, the most populous province in China, stated: "In the process of setting up a responsibility system for agricultural production, the Central Committee of the Chinese Communist Party and the Provincial Party Committee have repeatedly laid stress on proceeding from actual conditions and respecting the practice of the masses in building up socialist agriculture with Chinese characteristics."

In three years of practice, especially during the autumn of 1981, the family contract system became the main form of responsibility system and entered a phase of stabilization and gradual perfection. A survey conducted in November 1982 showed that among the 617,625 production teams in Sichuan Province, 89.2 percent had adopted the all-round household contract system; 8.8 percent the household output-contract system; and only 2 percent other forms of the responsibility system. Much the same took place on the national scene. According to a survey conducted in December 1982, 92 percent of China's production teams had adopted the contract system, of which 78.66 percent adopted the household contract responsibility system. The peasants like this straightforward system, since it allows them to keep what remains of their own produce after they fulfill the state purchase quotas and remit their contributions to the collective.

Household agricultural production occupies a sensitive position in Chinese history due to its close links with China's centuries-old feudal society. Feudal landowners rented their land in small plots, and thus there were very few big farms. Generation after generation, peasant households remained in one place tending small plots of land and engaging in related sideline occupations. This was the main form of small peasant production, and the reason Chinese feudal society endured for such a long time. In fact, household farming with the household as the unit of management engaging in diversified economic activities may be considered China's national form of farming. Chinese peasants have abundant experience in this kind of farming and a profound regard for it. As traditional forms of agriculture give way to modern ones, how to make best use of the national form has become a matter of considerable significance.

The household agriculture now practiced in China is fundamentally different from its past counterpart. Today's household contract farming is based on the premise that the land belongs to the collective. Its basic feature is the combination of a unified collective economy with scattered household production, which creates a new form of agricultural management. Socialist economic management may be instituted at several levels, one of which is the household level.

The combination of collective and individual responsibility in the household contract system is manifested in production, circulation and distribution. In the sphere of production, the collective takes care of water conservation facilities, farm machinery repairs, forecasting and prevention of crop diseases and pests, seed supply, etc. The contracting households are responsible for crop cultivation and field management. In regard to circulation, the collective economy organizes the supply of the means of production and purchases the major agricultural products, while the individual households may dispose of commodities not subject to state purchases. The peasants need not worry about marketing their produce, since this is provided for in their contracts with the collectives. As regards distribution, the contracting households turn over a fixed proportion of their income to the collectives to be used for collective undertakings and welfare for the disabled and aged. Since the greater part of the income remains with the individual peasants, they enjoy a fair degree of financial flexibility, and the principle of "those who work more get more" finds fuller expression.

Under the household contract system individual peasants are accumulating more means of production, such as oxen for plowing and small farm machines. A survey conducted in the provinces of Shanxi, Henan and Shaanxi showed that the number of oxen in the counties surveyed has increased by two or three times following the implementation of the household contract system, while the number of small farm machines has increased by three or four times. Significantly, many peasants are buying small tractors, a step on the way to the mechanization of Chinese agriculture.

The increase in individually owned production tools is a result of the peasants themselves planning the investment of funds in production. In the days of the "common pot", a considerable proportion of the funds went to defray the high expenses of the production team and most of what remained was used by the peasants for non-productive purposes. A portion of the funds is now reinvested in production. This is a positive change, and although the resulting increase in privately owned tools increases the scope of individual economy in the family contract system, there is no fundamental departure from the basic principle of combining individual production with collective management; thus it should be permitted and encouraged.

Experience has shown that the household contract system has changed the outlook of agricultural production and brought about marked improvements in the peasants' livelihood. In Chuxian County, Anhui Province, which adopted the household contract system at a relatively early date, gross production value in 1982 increased at a rate 7 percent greater than before the new system was instituted. Henan Province, which was among the first provinces to implement the new system, has achieved an extraordinary annual increase of 7.1 percent in agricultural production value, compared to the original 3.4 percent.

There are several reasons for the increased productivity under the household contract system. Besides offering incentives to the peasants, another important factor is that the system permits on-the-spot decision making. As we know, agricultural production deals with living things, the cultivation of which is determined not only by the amount of labor invested, but also by the timeliness and pertinence of such labor. Many decisions concerning such labor must be made on the spot. Before the household contract system came into practice, decisions were made exclusively by production team leaders. Agricultural production is a highly complex undertaking affected by such factors as crop variety, seed strains, soil conditions and the microclimate, and a production team leader cannot possibly know how each crop is growing on every spot of land at each stage of growth. This is why team leaders often gave incorrect instructions.

The household contract system has done away with this situation. Under this system, production is managed by the individual households which have the right to make their own decisions, thus eliminating blind direction and "remote control" in production. In practice, the household contract system is being improved continuously, and is becoming increasingly adaptable. It was once thought that the household contract system was more suitable for districts where agriculture was backward and where a single crop was produced. But good results have also been obtained when the system was instituted in areas with well-developed and more diversified economies. Some believed that the system could not be practiced in places with a high level of mechanization. Experience has shown that this is not true. Moreover, there has been an unexpectedly sharp rise in peasant purchases of farm machines either individually or with pooled funds.

How is it that the "overall household contract" system can

be instituted in economically developed areas? A report in the *People's Daily* (of January 23, 1983) explained that although these areas have a comparatively developed economy and fairly high level of mechanization, productivity is generally still quite low and the peasants are still essentially dependent on manual labor. Another *People's Daily* article on the Tangtou Brigade of Chuanfu Commune in Yixing County, Jiangsu Province, demonstrates that although irrigation, plowing, plant protection and threshing have been mechanized, machines only do 30 percent of the work, while the remaining farm work is still done by hand. Besides, whether in backward or developed areas, the "overall contract with the households" has a similar effect in countering the old practice of "eating out of the common pot".

The evolution of the household contract system has brought about a breakthrough in the theory of agricultural modernization. It was once thought that farms had to be large in order to provide room for developing the forces of production. Now it appears that modernization can be attained by small farms and even on the household scale, and that the modernization of production is not limited by the size of a farm.

2. Appearance of Specialized Households

As the household contract system spread, households specializing in a specific type of production began to appear, called "specialized households". Households which do some ordinary field work but spend most of their time on a single type of production are called "key households" or "semi-specialized households". "Specialized" or "semi-specialized households" are a natural outgrowth of rural economic development following the breakdown of agricultural by administrative fiat. From the very outset the specialized households were commodity producers. In this sense, they represent a new productive force which came into being through increased social division of labor rather than improved production tools. There are many skilled people in the countryside, some adept at raising livestock, others at firing bricks and tiles, blacksmithing, weaving, embroidering or other handicrafts. In the days when grain production was made the "key link" in agriculture, their special skills were unutilized. Now, under the new system, these skills are used to convert natural resources into a wide range of commodities to satisfy the peasants' needs. These new producers may be considered pioneers in the transformation of the natural economy in rural China into a commodity economy.

The diverse forms of production carried on by the specialized households have brought more goods to the country markets and more income to the peasants. Fundamentally speaking, this development fills an economic gap in the rural economy. Since the implementation of the Party's rural economic policies, though the peasants' incomes have increased, no qualitative changes have taken place in their lives. The peasants' increased bank deposits have engendered purchasing power directed at building houses and buying farm tools and clothing. This purchasing power and the commodity production and distribution systems which cater to it, are objective economic necessities;* the rural policies are simply the key that unlocked this long-forbidden area. Enlightening in this respect are the "Six 'Allows'" promulgated by Yichang Prefecture in Hubei Province in accordance with the spirit of the Central Government's policies: (1) allow individual rural manufacturers, traders and peasants skilled in stock raising to hire a certain number of assistants and apprentices within limits prescribed by the State Council; (2) allow them to dispose of their products after they have fulfilled state purchase quotas; (3) allow them to transport goods over long distances for marketing, and to specialize in such operations; (4) allow commune members to purchase farm machinery, trucks and boats; (5) allow commune members to re-allocate their contracted land on a voluntary basis so as to separate households specializing in grain production from those specializing in other forms of production;

---

* Some economists regard "economic necessities" as the necessities for use value.

and (6) further relax the restrictions on stock raising and timber and fruit tree cultivation and allow commune members to raise as much livestock and reclaim as much vacant land as they wish. The yield from reclaimed collectively-owned mountainous land goes to the commune members who reclaim it. Such land still belongs to the collective, but the commune members have the right to work it and the right of inheritance over anything of economic value they grow or raise on it. (This is necessary because timber and fruit trees take many years to produce economic returns.) Commune members may also refurbish their private mountain plots to develop forestry or to produce special mountain products. These "Six 'Allows' " are obviously designed to correct the erroneous "Leftist" policies of the past. They have released a tremendous burst of productive enthusiasm among the peasants and stimulated the long pent-up economic vitality of the masses.

The specialized households have developed faster than expected. Tai'an district in Shandong Province began to institute the household contract system in 1981, the year of the "big change". By autumn 1982, specialized or semi-specialized households numbered 230,000, or 13 percent of all households in the district. The national situation was much the same, with specialized or semi-specialized households accounting for 10 to 15 percent of the total.

Apart from the fundamental fact of economic necessity, another reason for the swift growth of the specialized households is their higher incomes. In 1982, the annual incomes of 186 households in Shifang County, Sichuan Province, reached the 10,000-yuan mark; all were specialized households.

Some obvious advantages of the specialized households, as revealed by an investigation in the above-mentioned Shifang County, can be defined as: (1) Better use of local resources. The local peasants do not leave an inch of land idle. They put all unused mountain slopes, bodies of water and river banks into production, and take meticulous care of their fields. One peasant family living high in the mountains took advantage of the environment to cultivate rare plants and flowers which find a ready market all over China; in 1982 this family earned 16,000 yuan. (2) Better use of manpower. A peasant in Longshe Commune in Shifang County skilled at bamboo weaving has enlisted the support of his whole family. He himself is in charge of planning, business relations, purchasing raw materials, designing products and selling them. His younger brother manages the family members in the weaving work; his father helps with the accounts and looks after the premises; and his mother does most of the housework. In 1982 they sold 4,000 yuan worth of goods. (3) Convenience in passing on traditional handicraft skills. An old man in Shifang County makes excellent bean curd. All four working members in his household have joined him in the venture, grinding the beans, boiling the bean milk, making the bean curd, and selling the final product. The family has prospered and the family tradition is carried on. Such household enterprises bring more income to the families, create wealth for society and enliven the rural economy.

From the social point of view, the most important function of the specialized households is the way they are breaking down the natural economy in the countryside and shifting the rural economy in the direction of a commodity economy. The result is an increasing division of labor in agricultural production, more varied commodity production, and a heightened sense of economic results among the peasants.

Specialized agriculture is inevitably socialized agriculture. Its development stimulates progress in all sectors of agriculture, as demonstrated by the following example: Ciyutuo Brigade in Liaozhong County, Liaoning Province has experienced a fairly rapid development of the specialized household system, with the majority of its 1,300 households now engaged in specialized production. Most of the land is cultivated by the 400 households which specialize in farming. Because these households are well provided with manpower, farm tools and farming experience, they obtain excellent harvests even in bad years. Like the other types of specialized households, these farming households have become part of the brigade's socialized production. This means that reforms of a revolutionary nature have taken place in the organization of agricultural production, reforms which highlight the role of agricultural planning and of the rural market. These reforms are engendering new problems, the solution of which will affect the nation's economic life, and entail the restructuring of the entire rural economic system.

3.   A New Social Stratum — Rural Inhabitants Detached from the Land

As groups of peasants become specialized in forms of production other than tilling the land, a new social stratum known as "peasants who have left the land but not the countryside" is emerging. Among them some still produce grain for their own consumption, but many no longer participate in agricultural production.

Such peasants, who leave the land by entire households, engage in the following types of production: 1) industries manufacturing building materials such as bricks, tiles, cement and glass; 2) traditional handicrafts such as blacksmithing, carpentry, stone masonry and bamboo weaving; 3) small-scale mining; 4) embroidery and weaving; 5) artistic handicrafts; 6) civil construction teams; 7) small processing enterprises servicing urban industries; 8) garment making; 9) trading; 10) service trades; and 11) other forms of labor service.

Apart from these specialized rural residents there are other peasants who have little land, or only small areas of water or mountainous land to work with, and engage in fishery, animal husbandry or forestry. All in all, about one-fifth of the rural labor force has become detached from the land to some degree. The surplus labor which once shared from the "common pot" now creates wealth for society.

A survey conducted in Dongguan County in Guangdong Province shows that more and more peasants have been leaving the land in recent years because of the rapid diversification of the economy. Nearly 120,000 of the county's 460,000 able-bodied workers, or one-third of the county's total rural labor force, have left farming. In one production brigade in Wanjiang Commune, only 367 of its 1,378 agricultural workers were working in the fields in 1982. They, plus another 39 engaged in forestry, pig raising and fishery, make up only 29 percent of the work force. The rest are now engaged in sideline production or service trades.

Among the peasants who have left the land are handicraftsmen who for years were not allowed to use their skills, and were compelled to work in production teams which did not need their labor in the first place. After the implementation of the new policies, these former handicraftsmen went back to their old trades and, moreover, took in considerable numbers of young people as apprentices. Handicraftsmen are in short supply in many rural areas, especially since the inception of the building boom and the increased demand for building materials and furniture. As a result, peasants who are skilled in handicrafts do not have time for farming, and have either turned over to others the land they had contracted to till or returned it to the production team. This benefits both the collective and themselves.

Some peasants are skilled in raising bees, marten and livestock. Such sidelines call for experience and skill and yield high incomes; thus it is only natural that a section of the peasantry should turn to these occupations.

Former rural cadres and middle school graduates are using the technical knowledge they obtain from newspapers and magazines to engage in specialized production, taking advantage of the abundant natural resources found in the countryside.

The possibility of obtaining greater economic benefits from non-agricultural production is a major reason why peasants leave the land. At first the peasants who spent the greater part of their time on sideline production still grew part of their food grain. Later, the production teams allowed them to remit a certain percentage of their income to the team and buy their food grain from the collective. Once they were able to establish stable businesses with regular incomes, these peasants began to devote all their time to specialized occupations. In the farming sector, too, the division of labor is tending toward specialization. Some peasants grow mainly grain crops and others economic crops. In these activities, the principle is to obtain the best economic results with the least labor, although of course not everyone realizes that his or her activities are governed by this principle.

A qualitative change is thus taking place as some of the peasant households turn to specialized production. Though they work in the areas of handicrafts, industry, commerce and services, they still live in the rural areas and receive their food grain from the production team.

These specialized households now play an increasingly important role in the economic life of society. According to a survey made in the outskirts of Shenyang, specialized hog-raising households which accounted for 14.6 percent of the rural population sold to the state 46 percent of the area's marketable hogs in 1982; and specialized chicken-raising households, accounting for 8.6 percent of the rural population, sold to the state 51 percent of the total number of eggs. In addition, these households also sold part of their produce on the market. This phenomenon deserves attention from the point of view of economic management and production organization, and ways should be sought to bring the specialized households' economic activities into step with the development of the rural economy as a whole. It should be noted that the present practice of specialized households turning in a certain amount of their income in return for food grain, fuel and other farm produce is only a transitional measure. The problem to be solved now is how to help them in production and provide them with proper management.

4.   New Types of Mergers

Further division of labor and increased specialization will inevitably result in the cooperation of households engaged in the same specialization. A survey report* from Shanxi Province shows that by the end of June 1982, 21,000 households in Xiaoliang Commune in Hejin County, accounting for 38 percent of the rural families and 38.5 percent of the work force, had joined such mergers. Fancun Commune had 282 mergers with 3,285 able-bodied workers or 32 percent of the work force. They engage in a wide variety of joint operations as follows:

1. Cooperative crop growing. Individual households still contract land from the production team but mark off adjoining strips to form a stretch of "grain tax" land on which they grow crops to fulfill state purchasing quotas and appropriations for collective funds. The cooperative team thus formed is collectively responsible for cultivating, managing and harvesting the crops, and for deliveries of the requisite amount of grain to the state purchasing station and the production team. The remaining contracted plots are plowed and sown collectively by the team but managed separately by each household, which eventually keeps all that is harvested on its own piece of land. Households growing economic crops also cooperate in such matters as seeds, employing new techniques and marketing.

2. Cooperation in animal raising. Several households may join forces to hatch chicks, operate stock breeding stations, or raise pigs, cows, fowl or marten.

3. Processing. Such mergers vary in size, depending on the distance and size of the cities in their vicinity and amount of work they contract from urban industries. Some commune members pool funds to buy tools for processing work; others purchase raw materials to produce locally needed goods, or use local natural resources or waste materials from big enterprises.

4. Cooperation in transportation. Joint transportation operations are quite common. About a dozen households pool funds to buy trucks, tractors, horse-drawn carts or boats for long dis-

---

* The authors of the survey are Wang Yunshan, Sun Chengnong and Zhang Xue.

tance transportation. Some combine transportation with trading. The scale and nature of such ventures vary considerably.

5. Cooperation in building. The boom in rural and urban housing construction in the last several years has given rise to building contracting teams which often include carpenters, blacksmiths, painters and electricians who work around a core group of masons and bricklayers. Such teams may consist of as many as a hundred persons.

6. Cooperation in forestry and fruit growing. Several households contract separately for tracts of mountain land and manage them jointly. The advantage of this kind of cooperation is that it permits a better combination of long- and short-term economic benefits and allows for flexibility in production.

7. Cooperation in handicrafts. Several households may jointly run lime or brick kilns or farm tool repair shops.

8. Cooperation in commerce and service trades. This may take the form of transporting and selling goods, operating teahouses, restaurants, inns, etc.

In addition to those mentioned above, there are some special cooperative entities:

1. Master-apprentice teams. A skilled handicraftsman may hire one or two assistants and several apprentices to form a small business.

2. Large-scale contractors for development projects. A commune member with technical and organizational skills may contract for an unused tract of mountain slope, waste land, or stretch of water, and cooperate with several others on its management. After turning in a certain amount of their income to the commune, the rest is divided among themselves according to the expertise and constribution of each worker. The contractor of the land or water area assumes responsibility for management and often gets a larger share of the profits. This is a new development in the countryside and is producing a big impact. The circumstances vary from one type to another and no ideal pattern has emerged.

3. Specialized service companies. Their services include seed supply, farm machinery, plant protection, chemical fertilizers

and agricultural techniques as well as follow-up services such as processing, transport and marketing. These companies, set up by the commune members themselves, are becoming a key link in agricultural production.

On the basis of these diverse combinations by specializations, another form of cooperation known as "chain" mergers has appeared in some places. These combine services handle all stages of farm production. Experiments in Guanghan County, Sichuan Province and elsewhere have provided models in this respect.

5. Fundamental Changes in the Agricultural Administrative System

It is evident that the above-described trend toward specialization and socialization in the rural economy is bound to have a deep effect on the administrative system in agriculture. In other words, the current system of "three-level administration by the commune, the production brigade and the production team, with the production team as the basic accounting unit" no longer suits the rural economy, and something new has to be devised.

Since the cooperative transformation of agriculture in the 1950s, China's rural economy, based on the production team as the basic accounting unit, has been modeled upon the collective farm system in the Soviet Union. The integration of government administration with economic management as practiced by the communes set up in 1958 has also proven to be inappropriate. And even then, the management methods of the production teams had not shaken off the influence of the Soviet collective farm system. Experience over the past years has shown that our management system has many defects; mainly, that "eating out of the common pot" restricts the initiative of the peasant masses. The present reforms taking place in the countryside are aimed at correcting this situation. The new forces of production and the new relations of production are shaking the old system, and the question of how to effect a planned and orderly reform of the commune system has now come to the fore.

As a matter of fact, the development of specialized cooperation already indicates the general direction of the reforms. With specialized cooperation as the basis, diverse forms of management will function for a long time, stimulating each other and developing side by side. Modes of production do not wither away before they run out of vitality; such is the case with household farming. It can be foreseen that agricultural management by family units will continue for a long time to come and specialized cooperation will exist in various forms and types and at many different levels. Under such circumstances, administration, management by planning, and market readjustment in the rural areas must be strengthened. At the same time, state enterprises — banks, industries and commercial departments — must step up their economic activities in the rural areas in order to help the rural economy develop under the guidance of state planning. Technical renovation is vital to economic reform, and technical service enterprises should intensify their efforts in the countryside. More intellectual investment and better education of young peasants in scientific farming are also indispensable to the advancement of the rural economy.

Another matter that requires consideration is the development of market towns, since these serve as a link between the rural and urban economies. Some of the present handicraftsmen who have left the land in recent years are active in the market town economy. Many rural inhabitants have set up restaurants, wineshops, stores and other services in the market towns, and their economic activities have become an important part of the market town economies. Thus, reconstructing the market towns to function as a regulator and link between the urban and rural economies is a matter of prime importance.

The growth of the rural commodity economy will inevitably be followed by an expansion of the rural market, and the development of rural commerce, including long-distance transport and trading, will in turn stimulate rural circulation and credit activities. This trend requires guidance from government departments, chiefly in the form of economic measures supplemented by administrative measures.

China's rural economy is now experiencing a transition from a natural economy to a commodity economy, and from traditional agriculture to modern agriculture. The creativity of the peasant masses has never manifested itself so vividly. Better guidance over, and further development of, the contract system are the key links in the reform of the rural economic system; they are also an irreversible trend. This once again proves that the prime factor in economic development is the forces of production. Present-day China is already assured of a rapid growth of the rural productive forces, and further reforms in the rural relations of production will inevitably follow.

Chapter VII

CHINESE RURAL ECONOMY — THE OUTLOOK

Since the establishment of the People's Republic of China in 1949, the development of the rural economy has proved the rationale that only socialism can fundamentally solve the question of Chinese agricultural development and the poverty of the peasants. The greatest transformation to have taken place in any period of Chinese history has paved the way for alleviating the food and housing problems of one billion people and for creating a Chinese type of socialism.

What is Chinese-type socialism? In order to answer this question, it is first necessary to analyze the overall situation in China. Viewed from the angle of the rural economy, China can be characterized by its large population and backward forces of production, with a labor force of over 300 million people, 72 percent of China's total social labor force. If the Chinese countryside is to become well off, it is necessary to control the rural population, thus enabling an increasing percentage of the rural labor force to free themselves from the natural (agricultural) and semi-natural economy, and engage in industrial production and other forms of labor. With this object, a strategy for all-round development to accord with conditions in China must be formulated on the basis of rural economic development.

Redirecting the rural labor force from agricultural production to industry and other lines of labor is a task of historic importance. History has shown that such a transformation often takes years to accomplish. In the course of this transformation, a portion of the agricultural labor force will engage in industrial labor and another portion in commerce and the service trades. For example, in a modern rural economy, the application of insecticides, indispensable to agricultural production, will no longer be handled by peasant families but by specialized insecticide service companies, thus influencing both the division of labor and the nature of the work itself. It is quite obvious that this can only follow upon major socio-economic changes, and as such is one element of the major social transformation that will be taking place in the Chinese countryside.

According to recent investigations, the rural population far exceeds the needs of agricultural production; in many places, roughly 25 to 30 percent may be considered surplus labor. This state of affairs is due to very complex reasons. Change can only be effected by finding new ways of production that can divert surplus labor onto paths leading to the creation of new wealth.

As industrialization is in the process of development in China, the absorption of surplus labor force by industry has great potential. Yet in view of the enormous labor resources in the villages, this potential is limited at present.

1. Comprehensive Development — The Only Way Out

The choice of pursuing comprehensive development in the rural economy is determined not only by the rural economy itself but also by the overall development of the social economy. Agriculture, in a broad sense, includes not merely crop cultivation but also animal husbandry, forestry, fishery, livestock and poultry raising, as well as industry, commerce, service trades and transportation. Cooperation and coordination between these areas is essential for the development of socialist agriculture. Apart from the division of labor and various forms of cooperation, socialist agriculture has yet another fundamental feature — its diversification.

Viewed as a whole, large-scale socialist agriculture is in direct contrast with single-crop agriculture, as is shown by the experiences of many developing countries. Only through the comprehensive development of agriculture can the social economy make significant progress. The difference lies in the fact that in a private-interest economy, the realization of comprehensive development pays the price of the bankruptcy and sacrifice of petty producers, often leading to a state of anarchy; whereas in large-scale socialist agriculture, steady advances can be attained by rational planning. In large-scale socialist agriculture, industry has its own particular role to play in the overall rural economy. In China, rural industry has increased year by year in terms of both size and production value. For example, Nantong County in Jiangsu Province had 79 industrial establishments in 1965. The number of such establishments increased to 1,268 in 1976, and to 2,171 in 1982. Production value in 1965 was 220,000 yuan, but reached 135.1 million yuan in 1976 and 517.6 million yuan in 1982. The 1982 figure showed an increase of 2,300 times compared with that of 1958, and an increase of 2.8 times over that in 1976.

The same report on Nantong County also revealed that in 1982, 13 million yuan was appropriated to aid agriculture in the county. These funds were drawn from the profits earned by the industrial establishments run by communes and production brigades and teams.

The development of rural industry has not only aided agriculture in financial terms. More important is the fact that it has unceasingly absorbed surplus farm labor as well. According to investigations conducted in Jiangyin, Wuxi and Yixing counties in Jiangsu Province, high population density (879 per sq. km.) and a scarcity of arable land resulted in each member of the agricultural population having, on the average, only 1.01 *mu* of arable land to farm. Under these conditions, there is bound to be plentiful surplus labor. The development of industry in the villages has led to significant improvements: in 1982, 39 percent of the rural labor force in the three counties was engaged in enterprises run by communes and production brigades and teams.

In southern Jiangsu Province, surplus labor is no longer a problem in many of the communes and production brigades and teams. The Huaxi Brigade in Jiangyin County is now affected by a shortage of labor, and has even absorbed labor from the neighboring communes and production brigades and teams. Another outstanding example is the Zhongxing Brigade in Haimen County. Situated along the Changjiang (Yangtze) River, the brigade has five production teams, a population of 826, with an average of 1.2 *mu* of arable land per capita. Recent efforts to develop brigade-run industrial, agricultural and sideline production have resulted in remarkable changes. The income of the brigade derived from industrial, agricultural, and sideline production in 1982 showed an increase of 4.2 times as compared with 1978. The proportion of industrial production value has increased to 89.5 percent, while that of agriculture production was only 5.5 percent and that of collective sideline production 5 percent. As for the labor force, 93 percent is engaged in industrial production and the remaining 7 percent in agricultural and sideline production. Due to a shortage of labor, more than 200 peasants from neighboring brigades take part in industrial production in the Zhongxing Brigade.

The object of industrial development in the countryside is, of course, not confined to structural changes in agricultural production and to the absorption of surplus labor. More important is the increase in social wealth.

At present, an extensive debate is taking place among Chinese economists as to the role of industry in the villages. Some are of the opinion that industrial production in the countryside is backward, that planning is insufficient, and that rural industrial development on a large scale will lead to an increase in small enterprises at the expense of large enterprises, as well as to competition for raw materials with large-scale industries in the cities. For these reasons they believe, it is necessary to limit the development of rural industries, confining their activities to obtaining raw materials from local sources, engaging in local manufacturing, and marketing their products locally. Judging from the actual situation in some rural industrial enterprises, this viewpoint is not without reason. In fact, some communes and production brigades and teams run their own enterprises at the cost of larger enterprises, and backward enterprises operate at the expense of advanced ones. In these places, urban industrial enterprises fail to operate at full capacity due to shortages of raw materials and energy, resulting in low production levels and substandard products. On the other hand, rural enterprises turning out high-cost products are in a better position as far as raw materials and energy is concerned. In terms of the overall economy, though, this is wasteful.

Other economists hold the view that, based on analyses of the majority of rural industrial enterprises, only a small number compete with the large-scale enterprises for raw materials and energy. In their view, the development of rural industry is inevitable in the development of the rural economy as a necessary adjunct to the industries in the cities. Competition from a small number of rural industrial enterprises for raw materials, energy and markets should not lead to restrictions on their development. This is a more convincing point of view.

In recent years, rural industries have developed extensively. According to investigations carried out in Jiangsu Province, there were 56,607 rural industrial enterprises in the province in 1982, with 3.43 million workers and a production value of 13,100 million yuan. In the counties under the jurisdiction of the city of Wuxi in the same province, there were 5,291 village industrial enterprises with more than 900 million yuan of fixed capital and over one billion yuan of floating capital. There were 116 enterprises each with more than 500 workers, annual production values of more than 10 million yuan, and annual profits of over one million yuan. These enterprises were involved in machine-making, metallurgy, chemical industry, textiles and building materials. The situation in Jiangsu is not unique; and it is predicted that in the future rural industries will play a growing role in the development of the Chinese economy.

Seen from present trends, the following types of enterprises will develop on a comparatively extensive scale: (1) those contracted by big industries in cities to process spare parts; (2) those operating with rehabilitated equipment formerly belonging to urban industrial enterprises; (3) those handling orders placed by state-operated commerce; (4) those engaged in processing work for, or supplying goods to, urban industries; (5) those which operate entirely on their own so far as obtaining raw materials, carrying out processing work and effecting sales locally; and (6) those relying on their own initiative for management, production and marketing, though they process customers' materials. These enterprises stand outside the centrally planned economy. Theoretically speaking, they come within the scope of the market economy and are a necessary adjunct to the socialist planned economy.

The development of rural sideline production has an important role to play in transforming the agricultural structure and in raising the peasants' living standards. The specialized production households and key production households emerging extensively in the countryside in recent years have, in fact, developed out of family sideline production. They are characterized by a high rate of commodity production, considerable incomes, and the ability to surplus agricultural labor. At present, they account for around 10 percent of all peasant households in China, though the figure is more than 30 percent in some places. In particular cases, entire villages are engaged in specialized production with only a small number of peasants active in agricultural production. In Nantong County, Jiangsu Province, some villages specialize in bamboo weaving, while others engage in sericulture or catch snakes. The development of sideline production in this area has created a flourishing rural economy.

In some villages which have undergone rapid development, measures have been taken to increase investments aimed at promoting education. Such investments will play a decisive role in transforming the rural economy, and well-to-do communes and production brigades and teams are required to contribute funds for this purpose. Well-developed rural areas need scientific knowledge to improve work in many fields; and rural areas embarking on the road of comprehensive development must emphasize socialized, specialized and commercialized production.

2. Diversification of the Agricultural Economy

The simultaneous existence of many forms of agricultural production is an important question in the development of agriculture. Across China's vast territory, some villages have basically freed themselves from the bondage of a natural economy, while others continue pursuing a natural or semi-natural economy. This unbalanced development, quite noticeable in the past, will continue unchanged for some time into the future. Under these circumstances, the Chinese rural economy will inevitably retain regional differences. Production relations and forms of management in the countryside will also remain diversified. Yet in spite of this diversity, China's socialist orientation and the system of socialist public ownership will not change.

Diversified agriculture can be discussed in three areas:

(1) Diversified agriculture implies agriculture administered under ownership at different levels, ownership referring to the extent of public ownership. Management systems must facilitate the development of production and promote the peasants' enthusiasm for production and for organizing economic work. Forms of production should suit the existing state of local productive force; consequently, the system of ownership by the whole people, the collective ownership system and the new forms of mergers will continue to coexist. This is especially so for the collective ownership system with its family contract-responsibility system, which will continue to manifest its superiority for a long period of time since it is directed at mobilizing the peasants' enthusiasm at the family level. Specialized production households, key production households and new forms of mergers — all which have come into being on the basis of the division of labor and division of production — will likewise coexist for a definite period of time. The new forms of mergers established on the basis of the socialist public ownership system will provide further forms of association and management, all suitable for agricultural development in the countryside. A case in point is the "merger of agriculture, industy and commerce" which has demonstrated great vitality in some areas.

In addition, other forms of economic associations should be encouraged, such as the joint selling of products from scattered households under contract and responsibility arrangements; technical cooperation on the basis of production by households under contracts; and cooperative information gathering by households engaged in specialized production.

Extended household contract production is another new form of cooperation. Attention should be paid, however, to the rational use of accumulation funds and payment of wages, so as to prevent any deviations from the correct path.

The small-scale individual economy is supplementary to the powerful socialist economy. There are reasons for its existence under specific conditions, and it must be protected in accordance with relevant policy. There exist in the countryside some households handling production entirely on their own. Their role in the development of agricultural production should be recognized; there is no reason why the small-scale individual economy should not be allowed to exist.

(2) Diversified agriculture implies agriculture with a technical structure which operates at different levels and in different forms. In some areas, mechanization and scientific farming has taken hold rapidly. For instance, in northeast China, state farms and agricultural cooperatives in the vicinity of the industrialized cities have mechanized most of their production. In other places, mechanization is confined to plowing, water conservancy, plant protection and the processing of agricultural products. In a considerable number of places, manual labor is still the general rule, while in a smaller number of places, farming is still done with the primitive method of slash-and-burn cultivation.

Diversified production can also be distinguished by the available sources of energy. In some places, electric power is used; other places rely on machine power; but in many places animal power is still widely used. There are also marked differences in the application of modern production techniques, such as the use of chemical fertilizers and insecticides and the planting of seeds. In dealing with these phenomena, applying uniform methods in all areas is a poor solution. Improvements must be effected gradually.

(3) Diversified agriculture also implies a great diversity of products. At present, China's agricultural sector is producing mainly raw materials; in terms of grain, it is mainly unprocessed grain which the peasants sell after fulfilling their state grain quotas. However, following improvements in production management and the development of the rural economy, various ways to process raw materials will be developed, leading to an increase in production value; examples of this include the first-stage processing of tea and silk reeling. Further trends in this direction must be promoted.

3. Integration of the Urban and Rural Economies

The integration of the urban and rural economies is important both theoretically and in guiding the work of rural economic reconstruction. Past practice demonstrates that handling complex economic relations by a system of administrative areas and administrative organs at different levels runs counter to the laws of economic activity. For this reason, it is necessary to set up economic zones centered around the large cities to link up the urban and rural economies. The system of giving the cities jurisdiction over the counties marks a step forward in this direction. This, however, is not enough. These city-county links must be further extended throughout the entire countryside, so as to create an urban-rural entity in the true sense of the term. This brings us to the function of the market towns, which have always occupied an important place in the history of the Chinese economy.

In the past 30 years, China's market towns have followed a twisted course marked by periods of both prosperity and depression. After the land reform and socialist transformation were carried out in the villages, a radical change took place in the character of the market towns; they became important bases where state-owned enterprises exercised leadership over the rural economy, at the same time serving as grassroots political, economic and cultural centers. As the new economic order evolved, state stores, supply and marketing cooperatives, banks, post offices and centers for the dissemination of modern production techniques were established, playing an important role in stimulating rural economic development.

The economic and social function of the market towns was totally abrogated during the ten years of the "cultural revolution". Market towns were revived following the downfall of the Gang of Four as part of the policy of stimulating the rural economy.

Market towns play an important role as centers of commodity circulation, and are often considered the primary markets for agricultural and sideline production. Because the socialist state economy cannot include all rural products in the state plan, the state must stimulate economic development by supplementary measures. The commercial functions of the market towns make significant contributions toward filling these gaps.

Another function of market towns is in the field of industry. Industry in market towns has, as a rule, been limited to handicrafts. A change occurred in the 1960s when, with the support of county-run industrial enterprises, small-scale service-related rural industrial enterprises (commune-run industries) appeared in the market towns. These enterprises were supported by agricultural income and appropriations from agricultural accumulation funds. They demonstrated the vitality of the newly emerging forms of socialist collective agriculture, and have been registering further development since the 1970s.

The third function of market towns lies in their serving as a channel through which socialist state economic organizations provide technical help and economic regulation to the countryside. This involves the establishment of financial organs, banks, post and telegraph offices, centers for disseminating technical information and industrial service centers. In sum, the market towns have an important role to play in the integration of the urban and rural economies, a function which does not present the threat of the countryside being exploited by the cities.

At present, there are over 50,000 market towns in China, with workers numbering several tens of millions. Some of them, known as "peasant-workers" live in villages, but do not subsist on commodity grain. Their work is performed mainly in market towns, though they also farm tiny grain plots. "Peasant-workers" constitute a social stratum in transition. In China, the turning of such labor from agriculture to industry will follow a rational course in that measures will be taken to create a model of Chinese-type industrialization. In the coming years, along with the increase in social production and the development of the urban and rural economies, we are bound to see further development of the market towns.

4. The Point of Departure of Modernization

The modernization of agriculture is one of the principal goals of socialist reconstruction in China. Considerable discussion on this subject has been taking place in academic circles, particularly regarding the point of departure. The conclusion is clear: agricultural modernization is conditioned upon social needs, and thus it must begin with the commercialization of agricultural products, the socialization of agricultural production and the redistribution of industrial funds on the basis of the division of labor and diversification of trades. Without these conditions, there will neither be motivation for agricultural modernization, nor a sound basis for its realization. Thus can be seen that the socialization of production is a decisive factor for agricultural modernization. We can even say that socialized production will lead to modernization, and that modernized production will in turn accelerate the socialization of production.

Agricultural modernization means (1) increasing the ratio of labor productivity and (2) increasing the ratio of productivity of the land. The former refers mainly to mechanizing agricultural work and utilizing electricity while the latter points to the application of modern methods for the increase of production, such as the application of chemical fertilizers and insecticides and the improvement of seed varieties. Owing to China's large territory and the complexities of its geography, population, sources of energy and economic conditions, it is absolutely impossible to adopt identical measures throughout the country.

At present, a considerable number of regions have implemented mechanized farming, irrigation, plant protection, water drainage and modern transport facilities, but only at low levels. Among the measures taken to increase production, the application of chemical fertilizers and insecticides is widespread, while in a small number of places, peasants are making use of herbicides. Viewing the overall situation, the level of modernization in China is not high. Further steps have to be taken with a view to a large-scale implementation of agricultural modernization. First, efforts should be made to develop industries turning out products for agricultural use to reduce their prices and make them profitable, necessary conditions for the peasants to be willing to invest in their purchase. Secondly, further efforts are necessary for the gradual transfer of the rural labor force to branches of production other than agriculture. Thirdly, efforts should be made to further enhance the level of production along lines of socialization, specialization and commercialization, with the object of increasing the peasants' income and their purchasing power for means of agricultural production. Fourthly, there should be further improvements made in the peasants' cultural, scientific and technical knowledge, and in the level of management of agricultural production. The specialization of production and commercialization of products now taking place in the rural economy are good indications of the present state of agricultural modernization. There is reason to believe that agricultural modernization in China will attain a comparatively high level by the end of the present century accompanied by a large-scale increase in agricultural production and in the level of rural economic reconstruction.

Chapter VIII

CONCLUSION

Having reviewed the development of China's rural economy, we have seen just how dramatic the changes of the past 30 or more years have been. During this period, the long-suffering peasants freed themselves from the shackles of the feudal landlord economy, and then organized themselves into mutual aid teams and cooperatives on the road to socialism. The Chinese peasants are no longer small property-owners but producers in a collective agriculture. Like industrial workers, they have become a fundamental force in China's socialist society; their labor is greatly respected in China's socialist economy; and they themselves are highly respected socialist workers. They are playing, and will surely continue to play, an enormous role in building China's future.

It is also evident that China's rural economy has taken a zig-zag road in its development. It experienced two major setbacks in the past 30 years, without which China's agriculture would have progressed at a much quicker pace. Both these setbacks show the baneful influence of "Leftist" thinking, which must now be eliminated to ensure steady progress in China's countryside.

Despite the setbacks and mistakes, the achievements in China's agriculture remain in the foreground. Peasants no longer rely on wild plants and chaff to tide them over the year, and although there are differences in income among the peasants, these are the outcome of different natural conditions and managerial ability rather than exploitation. Approximately 10 percent of the rural counties in China experience difficulties in production due to poor natural conditions. The implementation

169

of correct economic policies in recent years has brought about marked improvements in the livelihood and production of the peasants in these areas. The government also aids them by providing a variety of forms of direct assistance.

The rural economic policies implemented since the Third Plenary Session of the Eleventh Central Committee of the C.P.C. resulted in more rapid development of the peasants' sideline production. This is very important, since China has only a limited amount of arable land. Household sidelines provide work for surplus labor and make good use of untapped natural resources. Moreover, in areas where little technical equipment is available, household sidelines tend to concentrate on labor-intensive products. Under such circumstances, skilled labor can create much value even when raw materials are relatively scarce. At present, rural family sidelines account for 20 percent of the gross value of output in the agricultural sector.

Since the beginning of this decade, new economic policies have brought about striking changes in the countryside. The system of "linking payment to production and contracting by specialization" has done away with the practice of "eating from the common pot" and restored the vitality of the socialist cooperative economy. Once-stifled economic factors are being revived. Especially rapid development has been made by the household contract system, which has given new significance to the traditional form of organization — the household. But further efforts are needed to implement these policies thoroughly, particularly in view of the omnipresence of old conventions and conservative thinking. Important tasks facing us are to keep up ideological struggle and to uphold the policies set forth by the Third Plenary Session of the Eleventh Central Committee of the C.P.C.

It seems inevitable that the commune's "ownership at three levels with the production team as the basis" will be replaced by new forms of production organization. The system of integrating government administration with commune management no longer suits the present requirements of rural development.

Rural industry shows great promise, and is presently becoming an important link in an agricultural-industrial-commercial "chain". This means that farm products are processed locally and marketed by the peasants themselves — a departure from the old practice which kept the peasants from having any direct contact with the market. Experiments in various localities have demonstrated the effectiveness and vitality of this new system.

The spectrum of the present economic development is extremely broad. Under the premise of socialist public ownership, many forms of organization for agricultural production and a multi-layered socialist economy will coexist for some time to come. There has never been an entirely homogeneous social system in history, and socialism is no exception. The existence of many forms of economy in China is determined by the particularity of China's economic development.

Naturally, rapid population growth is a serious stumbling block to the development of the rural economy. The Chinese government has taken measures to curb the birth rate, including offering material incentives to couples who have only one child. Although the birth rate is declining, considerable effort must still be invested in this matter.

Generally speaking, China's rural economy has been making solid progress. It is now undergoing a transformation from a self-reliant or semi-self-reliant economy to a commodity economy, and from traditional to modern agriculture. This transformation must take place gradually. It is unrealistic to expect such a transformation to produce remarkable results in a short time, and it should be allowed to develop according to its own laws. Any subjective or unrealistic intervention will fail the test of practice. But one thing is certain: The great changes now being effected are entirely oriented to the needs of social development and conform to objective economic laws. We believe that if we persevere in our efforts and proceed from China's actual situation, we will be able to create a new model of development for China's rural economy to suit China's particular conditions and serve as a basis for the modernization of the national economy. A new socialist countryside in true Chinese style will be of increasing interest to the rest of the world.

POSTSCRIPT I

Complying with a request of the New World Press, I am glad to add the following supplementary remarks to what was said in the foregoing chapters.

I

The manuscript was completed in 1983. The figures contained herein are those available up to end of 1982. The reader may be interested to know what changes, if any, have occurred in the Chinese countryside since then.

There have been no changes in general policy. In fact, the policy as it stands today has been further developed. For instance, the principles guiding household contracts for the use of the land remain unchanged, though the terms of the contracts have been extended to more than 15 years. Why so long? This is because the peasants are, on the one hand, satisfied with their achievements and, on the other, apprehensive of a change in policy. The decision to implement 15-year terms encourages the peasants to make long-term investments in the land, which will result in a progressive increase in the returns.

Another important measure is the gradual concentration of land management in the hands of capable tillers. When a commune member under contract is unable to carry on tilling, or when he wants to terminate his contract or reduce its terms as he turns to another line of work, he may place the land in the hands of the collective, or transfer the contract to another person through consultation. He may not, however, change the terms of the contract concluded with the collective. In this way, the agricultural cooperatives can, under the joint production contract system, maintain and develop those advantages, technical or otherwise, which enhance agricultural production.

In addition, there has been a new emphasis on the process of commodity circulation. A flourishing economy with well developed agricultural and sideline production requires equally well developed commercial and transportation facilities; service trades connected with production are also very important. At present, these are weak links which call for strengthening.

II

The vigorous development of the rural economy in China has given rise to a series of typical questions which will be answered below:

One commonly asked question is: With the introduction of the household contract system, agricultural management lines, to all intents and purposes, with the peasant households; why is such management still described as socialist? This will be answered by stating three principles:

(1) The fundamental feature of socialist agriculture is the public ownership of the means of production. With the implementation of the large-scale contract system, land ownership in the villages remains unchanged: as the principal means of agricultural production, land remains under collective ownership. The households under contract have the right to use the land but not to own it. Moreover, production is by contract. This is markedly different in principle from distributing land to individuals.

(2) Under the contract system, households not only shoulder the responsibility of making maximum use of the land but are also obligated to make contributions to the collective accumulation fund and to fulfill state purchase quotas. Contributions to the collective accumulation fund also include agricultural tax payments, while the accumulation fund includes funds for public welfare. Accumulation funds are used in agricultural capital construction which lie beyond the capacity of individual households. Public welfare funds are used to provide for those

who can no longer work as well as the sick, the aged and the disabled.

(3) Although the contract system places the responsibility for agricultural management with the peasant households, this does not mean that the collective abstains entirely from such management. After the introduction of the contract system, the collective continues to participate in the management of production, but it will mainly manage mechanized plowing and seeding, water conservancy projects, irrigation crop and weather forecasts. What exists is actually a system of two-level management by the production team and the household. Under this system, the implementation of the contract system does not affect in the least the socialist collective economic system.

Another commonly asked question is: With the introduction of the contract system, land management rests with the household. Won't this lead to a situation detrimental to agricultural production? The answer to this question is simple. It was pointed out earlier that the concentration of land in the hands of capable tillers must be encouraged. In fact, this has already been carried out in the course of practice. With the extensive implementation of the household contract system, specialized production households and key production households have emerged in the villages. At the time of the preparation of this manuscript, there were 24.8 million households of these two types, representing 13 percent of all peasant households in China. Commodity production is predominant in household production. As a rule, specialized households develop industrial and sideline production first, followed by crop production. An increasing number of peasant households are engaged in specialized industrial and sideline production away from the farms, with the result that more and more specialized agricultural households manage farm production on a comparatively large scale. In some places, households assume the task of contract production of more than 100 *mu* of land. This trend suggests that the contract system will not bring about a scattering of land management, nor will benefits be lost through the large-scale implemention of the contract system.

A question more frequently asked is: Since the introduction of the contract system, the gap between economic incomes of peasant households has widened due to differences in management ability. Some peasant households have become well-to-do, particularly the specialized production households, with incomes exceeding that of other peasant households by one to more than ten times. This may lead to "polarization". What is the explanation for any such development? The problem here may lie in a confused conception of "polarization". As is generally known, "polarization" in the countryside was a product of the private ownership of land. Some petty producers became well-to-do, bought land and hired labor, while others lost their land and became hired laborers. This is what "polarization" implies. The present prosperity of certain peasants is not based on such exploitative relations. There are only differences in the time it takes for the peasants to become rich. We stand for common prosperity, not egalitarianism, which is both impossible to achieve and unscientific. Efforts to bring about egalitarianism are detrimental to the development of production.

Another question is: Is the transfer of the contract system from the commune to the peasant household a retrogression? The answer is a resolute "No". After the communes ceased handling administrative affairs, agricultural cooperative management organizations based on the production brigades or teams were set up extensively. The production teams are separated from the village administration, but remain part of the agricultural cooperatives, and are responsible for concluding production contracts with peasants. The original communes have become village administrations and joint agricultural cooperatives. The former are administrative organs, while the latter are agricultural enterprises belonging to the collective ownership system. These arrangements can invigorate the development of the rural productive forces without the evils of administrative interference and arbitrary and impracticable directive. They are an aid in mobilizing the initiative of the peasants and in expanding the economic potential of the collective economy. This situation cannot possibly be regarded as a retrogression.

Yet another question is: Will the mechanization of agricultural production be handicapped by the household production system? Practice has shown that the answer is "No". After the introduction of the responsibility system in the countryside, the process of mechanization has not been brought to a halt but further developed. In 1978, according to statistics, the total motive power of farming machinery was 159 million horsepower; in 1982, it was 225 million horsepower. Big and medium tractors numbered 557,000 in 1978 and 821,000 in 1982. Small tractors totaled 1.37 million in 1978 and 2.30 million in 1982. The power capacity of irrigation and drainage machinery increased from 65.77 million horsepower in 1978 to 76.03 million horsepower in 1982. The number of tractors purchased by households individually or jointly throughout the country now totals 1.20 million. The number of such purchases in Guangdong, Guangxi, Fujian, Qinghai, Ningxia and Anhui provinces account for more than 50 percent of all the tractors in these provinces and autonomous regions.

III

I would like here to express my deep gratitude to Professor Fei Hsiao Tung, who kindly wrote the preface to this book. His words of encouragement have always inspired me to make greater efforts in my work.

I am greatly indebted to Comrades He Renrui and Xiao Yiwei for their assistance in organizing much of the statistical information in this book, as well as to all those who took part in the work of translation, without which the publication of this book would have been impossible.

Luo Hanxian

Beijing,
February 1984

POSTSCRIPT   II

Even as this book is going to press, new developments have made it necessary to reassess some of the ideas suggested in the book and bring them up to date. In this postscript I will confine my attention only to the major areas in which changes have occurred recently. They include:

(1) *The concentration of land.* An initial result of the introduction of the responsibility system, before the appearance of the "specialty households", was a countrywide distribution of land. In some cases the measure was carried to such an extreme that to provide an equitable distribution of good and poor land, fields were broken up into small pieces. But as the system developed there was a complete reversal of this trend. More and more farmers were willing to give up their land and devote their time to small businesses, while others, usually experienced cultivators, were eager to work the additional land. This convergence of land into the hands of the most capable farmers has proven beneficial both to agricultural production and to the growth of small businesses in the countryside. Encouraged by government policies, and particularly the 15-year tenure, this trend is gaining momentum. Apart from the above-mentioned abandoned land, the redistribution also includes lands formerly in reserve, the lands under unified management for feeding five-guarantee households, and lands of short-handed households. The redistribution of land provides a new grain-producing network upon which the state can depend for public grain and for sales of surplus grain. In national terms this tendency will add to the success of the "some peasants get rich first" policy as peasants growing grain

and commercial crops prosper along with the specialty house-holds in other lines.

(2) *Rapid industrialization.* It is noteworthy that in some of the faster-developing rural economies joint agro-industrial units, or, on a higher level, industries, are beginning to play a major role. Daqiu Village, in Jinghai County of Tianjin, is a perfect example. Economically underdeveloped in the past, it has been increasing its commitment to industry until 90 percent of its labor force and 95 percent of the value of its total output are in the industrial sector. The changing situation in rural industry is also apparent in the shift from a narrow, local emphasis to a much broader and more progressive one. Formerly crippled by the self-imposed policy of "three locals" (local resources, local manufacture and local use), rural businesses have now begun to set their sights on the national and even international market, while cooperating with urban industry and research institutes in an effort to diversify their products. Now foreign technology is imported and patents are bought. All this has helped the small-scale but flexible rural industry come into its own.

(3) *Improvement of channels for the circulation of commodities.* In this respect mention should first of all be made of the reform efforts in the management of cooperatives. Privately financed cooperatives, originally grassroots commer-cial organizations, were gradually bureaucratized and lost their value as a conveyance of grassroots will. Now long-awaited improvements are taking place as reform of the cooperatives has been placed on the national agenda. In cases where such reforms have already taken place, reorganization and de-centralization have had a decisive impact on the circulation of commodities.

Another important aspect of the reforms of the system of circulation of commodities is the trend towards a multi-level and multi-channel system. Once regarded as "peasants de-viating from their traditional field of work," country peddlers for instance, have been taken back into the mainstream economy. Though their capital is small, their numbers are great. Their presence in almost all areas has enhanced the circulation of commodities and played its role as a vital subsidiary economic force.

Special notice should be taken of the farm produce wholesalers markets, incorporating mainly state businesses. They are designed to provide an arena for transactions of businesses regardless of their different sizes and different types of ownership. These markets are suited to the unpredictable character of agricultural production and the present conditions in which communications and the dissemination of information are limited and the governmental planning system is not entirely perfect.

(4) *Urbanization of the countryside.* Not too long ago when "leftist" ideas were rampant, urbanization was viewed with prejudice, sometimes to such an extent that it was practically equated with capitalism. As a result "new peasant villages" were forced upon many economically unprepared areas in an attempt to realize the mistaken concept of a "transition in poverty". Now, a changed conception has triggered a chain of other changes. Urbanization is regarded as a natural outcome of economic development. The population flow into rural towns is seen as providing a labor force which helps promote the prosperity of these small towns, which in turn provide technology, information, capital and a market for the surrounding countryside.

(5) *Investment market.* With the current economic growth there are indications that peasant capital surpluses are being invested in other businesses. In response investment companies and "development centers" have sprung up. It is too early to predict the course they will follow and how they will be handled by the administration of industry and commerce, but these developments are a sign of rural prosperity and are contributing to increased growth in the countryside.

(6) *Impact of rural reforms on the urban economy.* Many variations of the responsibility system are now being tried out on the urban economic system. A form of management known as "keeping a grip on the most important while letting go of

the rest", for instance, has been adopted in some towns to give more freedom to enterprises. Other state-owned businesses are managed collectively, assuming responsibility for their own profits and losses. Bold experiments are being performed in the building industry, not only in management but also in the introduction of a new wage system in which salaries are linked directly with output value.

These reforms are a necessary part of a fast-developing commodity economy. Given the current situation, we can be confident that China's rural economy will continue to press ahead to brighter future prospects through continued reform.

Luo Hanxian

Beijing
August 1984

Appendices

DEVELOPMENT OF AGRICULTURAL
COLLECTIVIZATION IN CHINA

Agricultural Mutual Aid Teams
(1950-1956)

(in millions)

	Number of mutual aid teams	Number of partic- ipating households
1950	2.724	11.313
1951	4.675	21.0
1952	8.03	45.364
1953	7.45	45.637
1954	9.931	68.478
1955	7.147	60.389
1956	0.85	1.042

(All figures in the appendices were supplied by State Statistical Bureau)

Agricultural Producers' Cooperatives
(1950-1957)

	1950	1951	1952	1953	1954	1955	1956	1957
Cooperatives (in thousands)	19*	130*	4	15	114	634	756	789
Advanced co-ops (in thousands)	1*	1*	10*	15*	0.2	0.5	540	753
Elementary co-ops (in thousands)	18*	129*	4	15	114	633	216	36
Participating households (in thousands)	219*	1,618	59	275	2,297	16,921	117,829	121,052
Advanced co-ops (in thousands)	32*	30*	2	2	12	40	107,422	119,450
Elementary co-ops (in thousands)	187*	1,588*	57	273	2,285	16,881	10,407	1,602
Average number of households per co-op	11.5	12.4	16.2	18.2	20.1	26.7	155.9	153.4
Advanced co-ops	32.0	30.0	184.0	137.3	58.6	75.8	198.9	158.6
Elementary co-ops	10.4	12.3	15.7	18.1	20.0	26.7	48.2	44.5

NOTE: All figures marked with the asterisk are the actual numbers, to which the remark "in thousands" does not apply.

Rural People's Communes
(1958-1979)

	Number of communes	Number of production brigades (in millions)	Number of production teams (in millions)	Number of households in communes (in millions)	Number of commune members (in millions)
1958	23,630			128.61	560.17
1959	25,450	0.518	3.299	127.45	554.43
1960	24,317	0.464	2.892	126.62	
1961	57,855	0.734	4.089	131.99	
1962	74,771	0.703	5.530	134.10	
1963	80,956	0.652	5.643	134.24	568.33
1964	79,559	0.644	5.590	133.88	575.72
1965	74,755	0.648	5.412	135.27	591.22
1966	70,278	0.651	5.164	136.61	606.48
1967	70,050	0.649	5.106		
1968	59,812	0.641	4.869		
1969	53,722	0.648	4.585		
1970	51,478	0.643	4.564	151.78	699.84
1971	52,674	0.654	4.587	153.87	716.11
1972	53,823	0.662	4.722	156.01	731.81
1973	54,423	0.667	4.769	158.39	747.98
1974	54,620	0.671	4.800	161.39	763.89
1975	52,615	0.677	4.826	164.48	777.12
1976	52,665	0.681	4.827	168.03	787.45
1977	52,923	0.683	4.805	171.07	796.88
1978	52,781	0.690	4.816	173.47	803.20
1979	53,348	0.699	5.154	174.91	807.39

TOTAL ANNUAL VALUE OF INDUSTRIAL AND AGRICULTURAL PRODUCTION (1949-1982)

(Selected Years)

(Unit: billion RMB yuan)

	Total value of industrial and agricultural production	Total value of agricultural production
(Calculated according to 1952 fixed prices)		
1949	466	326
1952	827	484
1957	1,388	604
(Calculated according to 1957 fixed prices)		
1959	1,241	537
1962	1,280	430
1965	1,984	590
(Calculated according to 1970 fixed prices)		
1978	5,690	1,459
1979	6,175	1,584
1980	6,619	1,627
1981	6,919	1,720
(Calculated according to 1980 fixed prices)		
1981	7,490	2,369.2
1982		2,629.2

AREA OF GRAIN GROWING LAND (1949-1982)

(Unit: million *mu*)

	Total grain crops	Rice	Wheat
1949	1,649.38	385.63	322.73
1950	1,716.09	392.24	342.00
1951	1,766.53	404.00	345.82
1952	1,859.68	425.73	371.70
1953	1,899.55	424.82	384.54
1954	1,934.92	430.83	404.51
1955	1,947.59	437.60	404.09
1956	2,045.09	499.68	409.08
1957	2,004.50	483.62	413.13
1958	1,914.20	478.73	386.63
1959	1,740.34	435.51	353.62
1960	1,836.44	444.11	409.41
1961	1,821.65	394.14	383.58
1962	1,824.31	404.02	361.13
1963	1,811.12	415.73	356.57
1964	1,831.55	444.10	381.12
1965	1,794.41	447.37	370.64
1966	1,814.82	457.93	358.78
1967	1,788.45	456.54	379.49
1968	1,742.36	448.41	369.87
1969	1,764.06	456.48	377.43
1970	1,789.01	485.37	381.87
1971	1,812.69	523.77	384.59
1972	1,818.14	527.14	394.53
1973	1,817.34	526.35	396.58
1974	1,814.64	532.68	405.92
1975	1,815.93	535.93	414.91
1976	1,811.15	543.26	426.26
1977	1,806.00	532.89	420.98
1978	1,808.81	516.31	437.74
1979	1,788.94	508.09	440.35
1980	1,758.52	508.18	438.42
1981	1,724.37	499.42	424.60
1982	1,700.94	495.84	419.12

ANNUAL GRAIN PRODUCTION (1949-1982)

(Unit: million metric tons)

	Total grain production	Rice	Wheat
1949	113.18	48.65	13.81
1950	132.13	55.10	14.49
1951	143.69	60.56	17.23
1952	163.92	68.43	18.13
1953	166.83	71.27	18.28
1954	169.52	70.85	23.34
1955	183.94	78.03	22.97
1956	192.75	82.48	24.80
1957	195.05	86.78	23.64
1958	200.00	80.85	22.59
1959	170.00	69.37	22.18
1960	143.50	59.73	22.17
1961	147.50	53.64	14.35
1962	160.00	62.99	16.67
1963	170.00	73.77	18.48
1964	187.50	83.00	20.84
1965	194.53	87.72	25.22
1966	214.00	95.39	25.28
1967	217.82	93.69	28.48
1968	209.06	94.53	27.46
1969	210.97	95.06	27.29
1970	239.96	109.99	29.19
1971	250.14	115.21	32.58
1972	240.48	113.36	35.99
1973	264.94	121.74	35.23
1974	275.27	123.91	40.87
1975	284.52	125.56	45.31
1976	286.31	125.81	50.39
1977	282.73	128.57	41.08
1978	304.77	136.93	53.84
1979	332.12	143.75	62.73
1980	320.56	139.91	55.21
1981	325.02	143.96	59.64
1982	353.43	161.25	68.42

ANNUAL PER *MU* GRAIN PRODUCTION (1949-1982)

(Unit: kilogram)

	Total grain production	Rice	Wheat
1949	68.5	126	43
1950	77	145.5	42.5
1951	81.5	150	50
1952	88	161	49
1953	88	168	47.5
1954	87.5	164.5	57.5
1955	94.5	178.5	57.5
1956	94	165	60.5
1957	97.5	179.5	57
1958	104.5	169	58.5
1959	97.5	159.5	62.5
1960	78	134.5	54
1961	81	136	37
1962	87.5	156	46
1963	94	177.5	52
1964	102.5	187	54.5
1965	108.5	196	68
1966	118	213.5	70.5
1967	122	205	75
1968	120	211	59
1969	119.5	207.5	73
1970	134	226.5	76.5
1971	138	220	84.5
1972	132.5	215	91
1973	141	231.5	89
1974	151.5	232.5	100.5
1975	156.5	234.5	109
1976	158	231.5	118
1977	151.5	241.5	97.5
1978	168.5	265	123
1979	185.5	283	142.5
1980	182	275	125
1981	188.5	288	140.5
1982	208	325	163

AREA OF PRINCIPAL ECONOMIC CROPS (1949-1982)

(Unit: million *mu*)

	Cotton	Oil-bearing crops	Jute and hemp	Sugar cane	Beetroot
1949	41.55	63.42	0.43	1.62	0.24
1950	56.79	62.65	0.73	1.69	0.31
1951	82.27	77.18	2.66	2.12	0.35
1952	83.64	85.71	2.37	2.74	0.53
1953	77.70	80.42	1.19	2.89	0.73
1954	81.93	86.49	1.08	3.28	1.10
1955	86.59	102.56	1.74	3.06	1.72
1956	93.83	102.40	2.06	3.32	2.24
1957	86.63	103.98	2.14	4.00	2.39
1958	83.34	95.35	1.78	4.58	4.34
1959	82.68	92.24	1.82	4.71	4.75
1960	78.37	86.90	1.70	4.65	5.21
1961	58.05	63.59	0.99	2.83	3.10
1962	52.46	62.30	0.93	2.31	1.25
1963	66.14	68.20	1.13	2.76	1.17
1964	74.03	79.09	1.26	4.59	1.87
1965	75.05	77.50	1.70	5.26	2.56
1966	73.88		2.62	5.18	2.91
1967	76.47		2.65	5.13	2.77
1968	74.79		2.22	4.81	2.55
1969	72.44		2.09	4.92	2.78
1970	74.95	67.83	2.02	5.81	2.98
1971	73.85	71.87	1.98	6.39	3.29
1972	73.44	79.45	2.51	7.15	3.99
1973	74.13	79.87	3.75	7.57	4.28
1974	75.20	79.89	4.31	7.39	4.00
1975	74.33	84.78	4.46	7.85	4.54
1976	73.94	86.81	4.93	8.12	5.35
1977	72.67	84.59	5.65	7.60	5.28
1978	73.00	93.34	6.18	8.23	4.96
1979	67.68	105.77	5.43	7.68	4.88
1980	73.80	118.93	4.71	7.19	6.64
1981	77.78	137.01	4.59	8.27	6.54
1982	87.43	140.15	3.69	9.80	6.93

PER *MU* PRODUCTION OF PRINCIPAL
ECONOMIC CROPS (1949-1982)

(Unit: kilogram)

	Cotton	Oil-bearing crops	Jute and hemp	Sugar cane	Beetroot
1949	11	40.5	86.5	1,627.5	797
1950	12	47.5	108.5	1,858.5	783
1951	12.5	47	94	2,181	1,023.5
1952	15.5	49	129	2,600	909.5
1953	15	48	116	2,499	642
1954	13	50	126.5	2,618.5	903
1955	17.5	47	147.5	2,647.5	926.5
1956	15.5	49.5	125	2,610	734.5
1957	19	40.5	141	2,599	628
1958	23.5	50	150.5	2,742	709
1959	20.5	44.5	124.5	1,907	667.5
1960	13.5	22.5	119	1,778	306.5
1961	14	28.5	124	1,508	256.5
1962	14.5	32	142.5	1,492.5	271
1963	18	36	175.5	2,827.5	445.5
1964	22.5	42.5	186.5	2,648.5	698
1965	28	47	164.5	2,548	774
1966	31.5		133.5	2,202	904
1967	31		150	2,440.5	938
1968	31.5		178	2,149	846.5
1969	28.5		164.5	2,134	857.5
1970	30.5	55.5	169	2,315	705
1971	28.5	57	153.5	2,057	645.5
1972	26.5	52	151	2,294.5	582
1973	34.5	52.5	148.5	2,240.5	626
1974	33	55.5	146	2,224	572.5
1975	32	53.5	157	2,122	546
1976	28	46	148.5	2,049.5	548.5
1977	28	47.5	152.5	2,335	467
1978	29.5	56	176	2,556.5	544.5
1979	32.5	61	201	2,802	637
1980	36.5	64.5	233	3,170.5	949.5
1981	38	74.5	274.5	3,588	973
1982	41	84.5	287.5	3,703.5	968

TOTAL ANNUAL PRODUCTION OF PRINCIPAL ECONOMIC CROPS (1949-1982)

(Unit: million metric tons)

	Cotton	Oil-bearing crops	Jute and hemp	Sugar cane	Beetroot
1949	0.4444	2.5635	0.0368	2.6421	0.1905
1950	0.6924	2.9720	0.0788	3.1334	0.2449
1951	1.0305	3.6200	0.2497	4.6289	0.3600
1952	1.3037	4.1931	0.3055	7.1158	0.4785
1953	1.1747	3.8555	0.1379	7.2090	0.5051
1954	1.0649	4.3050	0.1366	8.5923	0.9890
1955	1.5184	4.8265	0.2568	8.1100	1.5961
1956	1.4451	5.0855	0.2577	8.6546	1.6459
1957	1.6400	4.1959	0.3009	10.3924	1.5010
1958	1.9687	4.7695	0.2674	12.5526	3.0775
1959	1.7088	4.1040	0.2260	8.9793	3.1682
1960	1.0629	1.9405	0.2019	8.2583	1.5965
1961	0.8000	1.8135	0.1226	4.2681	0.7967
1962	0.7500	2.0033	0.1321	3.4433	0.3387
1963	1.2000	2.4584	0.1983	7.8014	0.5194
1964	1.6627	3.3684	0.2349	12.1607	1.3040
1965	2.0977	3.6253	0.2792	13.3914	1.9843
1966	2.3367		0.3493	11.4082	2.6269
1967	2.3539		0.3977	12.6403	2.6011
1968	2.3543		0.3955	10.3409	2.1547
1969	2.0793		0.3438	10.4968	2.3863
1970	2.2770	3.7718	0.3413	13.4570	2.1027
1971	2.1047	4.1130	0.3035	13.1387	2.1251
1972	1.9581	4.1176	0.3785	16.4163	2.3223
1973	2.5617	4.1863	0.5579	16.9645	2.6784
1974	2.4607	4.4142	0.6298	16.4324	2.2885
1975	2.3808	4.5207	0.6993	16.6668	2.4763
1976	2.0554	4.0078	0.7307	16.6307	2.9322
1977	2.0487	4.0174	0.8612	17.7523	2.4062
1978	2.1670	5.2179	1.0877	21.1164	2.7023
1979	2.2073	6.4353	1.0894	21.5075	3.1058
1980	2.7067	7.6905	1.0984	22.8074	6.3053
1981	2.9676	10.2052	1.2601	29.6681	6.3603
1982	3.5984	11.8173	1.0603	36.8824	6.7115

FORESTED AREA (1950-1982)

(Unit: million *mu*)

	Forested area		Forested area
1950	1.899	1967	58.560
1951	6.765	1968	21.200
1952	16.280	1969	52.190
1953	16.694	1970	58.260
1954	17.493	1971	67.877
1955	25.658	1972	69.536
1956	95.849	1973	74.743
1957	65.326	1974	75.037
1958	91.480	1975	74.606
1959	81.745	1976	73.886
1960	62.159	1977	71.899
1961	21.620	1978	67.445
1962	17.981	1979	67.339
1963	22.952	1980	68.280
1964	43.670	1981	61.650
1965	51.384	1982	67.434
1966	68.000		

YEAR-END TOTALS OF LARGE ANIMALS
IN PENS (1949-1982)

(Unit:　million　head)

	Total of large animals	Cattle	Horses	Donkeys	Mules	Camels
1949	60.02	43.936	4.875	9.494	1.471	0.247
1950	65.38	48.103	5.217	10.317	1.497	0.246
1951	70.44	52.088	5.486	11.016	1.353	0.266
1952	76.46	56.600	6.130	11.806	1.637	0.285
1953	80.76	60.083	6.512	12.215	1.645	0.301
1954	85.30	63.623	6.939	12.700	1.717	0.320
1955	87.75	65.951	7.312	12.402	1.723	0.357
1956	87.73	66.601	7.372	11.086	1.711	0.363
1957	83.82	63.612	7.302	10.864	1.679	0.365
1958	77.68	59.069	6.893	9.773	1.571	0.373
1959	79.12	61.094	7.058	9.030	1.547	0.387
1960	73.36	57.443	6.585	7.527	1.427	0.381
1961	69.49	55.005	6.211	6.565	1.332	0.378
1962	70.20	55.717	6.320	6.454	1.324	0.386
1963	75.05	59.680	6.865	6.746	1.355	0.402
1964	79.43	63.158	7.394	7.048	1.403	0.425
1965	84.21	66.951	7.921	7.438	1.447	0.448
1966	87.40					
1967	89.82					
1968	91.79					
1969	92.28					
1970	94.36	73.583	9.648	8.400	2.245	0.487
1971	95.37	73.986	9.926	8.513	2.444	0.505
1972	95.76	73.866	10.341	8.353	2.682	0.515
1973	97.18	74.676	10.730	8.350	2.923	0.500
1974	97.53	74.554	11.103	8.233	3.139	0.504
1975	96.86	73.547	11.299	8.127	3.354	0.535
1976	94.98	71.693	11.438	7.766	3.536	0.545
1977	93.75	70.398	11.447	7.630	3.715	0.564
1978	93.89	70.724	11.245	7.481	3.868	0.574
1979	94.59	71.346	11.145	7.473	4.023	0.604
1980	95.25	71.676	11.042	7.748	4.166	0.614
1981	97.64	73.301	10.972	8.415	4.325	0.628
1982	101.13	76.073	10.981	8.999	4.464	0.610

YEAR-END TOTALS OF PIGS, SHEEP
AND GOATS IN PENS (1949-1982)

(Unit: million head)

	Pigs	Sheep and goats
1949	57.75	42.35
1950	64.01	46.73
1951	74.40	52.87
1952	89.77	61.78
1953	96.13	72.02
1954	101.72	81.30
1955	87.92	84.22
1956	84.03	91.65
1957	145.90	98.58
1958	138.29	95.68
1959	120.42	111.65
1960	82.27	112.81
1961	75.52	123.87
1962	99.97	134.65
1963	131.80	137.47
1964	152.47	136.69
1965	166.93	139.03
1966	193.36	138.08
1967	190.06	144.33
1968	178.63	144.21
1969	172.51	140.21
1970	206.10	147.04
1971	250.35	150.11
1972	263.68	149.32
1973	257.94	157.28
1974	260.78	160.87
1975	281.17	163.37
1976	287.25	158.17
1977	291.78	161.36
1978	301.29	169.94
1979	319.71	183.14
1980	305.43	187.31
1981	293.70	187.73
1982	300.78	181.79

ANNUAL AQUATIC PRODUCTION (1949-1982)

(Unit: million metric tons)

	Annual production		Annual production
1949	0.448	1966	3.098
1950	0.912	1967	3.052
1951	1.332	1968	2.711
1952	1.666	1969	2.899
1953	1.900	1970	3.185
1954	2.294	1971	3.496
1955	2.518	1972	3.842
1956	2.648	1973	3.931
1957	3.116	1974	4.282
1958	2.811	1975	4.412
1959	3.089	1976	4.476
1960	3.038	1977	4.695
1961	2.305	1978	4.656
1962	2.283	1979	4.305
1963	2.614	1980	4.497
1964	2.804	1981	4.606
1965	2.984	1982	5.155

YEAR-END TOTALS OF PRINCIPAL
FARM EQUIPMENT (1952-1982)

(Selected Years)

(I)

	Total horsepower of farm equipment (million h.p.)	Large- and medium-sized tractors	Walking tractors
1952	0.25	1,307	
1953	0.42	1,582	
1954	0.54	2,945	
1955	0.72	4,767	
1956	1.26	11,267	
1957	1.65	14,674	
1958	3.42	26,396	
1959	5.47	33,289	
1960	8.01	45,536	
1961	9.11	52,239	
1962	10.29	54,938	919
1963	11.48	59,235	992
1964		65,868	1,294
1965	14.94	72,599	3,956
1970	29.44	125,498	73,309
1971		150,179	133,550
1972		189,944	207,731
1973	65.03	234,078	302,177
1974	80.63	280,676	421,223
1975	101.68	344,518	598,533
1976	117.33	397,000	825,000
1977	139.52	467,000	1,091,000
1978	159.75	557,358	1,373,000
1979	181.91	666,823	1,671,000
1980	200.49	744,865	1,874,000
1981	213.59	789,000	2,037,000
1982	225.89	812,447	2,287,000

YEAR-END TOTALS OF PRINCIPAL
FARM EQUIPMENT (1952-1982)

(Selected Years)

(II)

	Combine harvesters	Irrigation and drainage machinery	
		Units (in millions)	Horsepower (million h.p.)
1952	284		0.128
1953	429		0.141
1954	591		0.164
1955	943		0.208
1956	1,451		0.385
1957	1,789	0.040	0.564
1958	3,452		1.640
1959	4,908		3.126
1960	5,857		4.814
1961	6,245	0.312	5.368
1962	5,906	0.367	6.147
1963	6,001	0.415	6.934
1964	6,176	0.448	7.585
1965	6,704	0.558	9.074
1970	8,002	1.471	18.249
1971	8,685	1.640	19.848
1972	9,399	2.078	24.645
1973	9,164	2.880	34.621
1974	10,901	3.422	40.865
1975	12,551	3.891	48.666
1976	14,233	4.262	54.166
1977	15,732	4.695	60.046
1978	18,987	5.026	65.575
1979	23,026	5.384	71.221
1980	27,045	5.630	74.645
1981	31,268	5.672	74.983
1982	33,904	5.803	76.697

YEAR-END TOTALS OF PRINCIPAL FARM EQUIPMENT (1957-1982)

(Selected Years)

(III)

| | Trucks for farm use (units) | Motorboats for fishery | |
		Units	Horsepower (million h.p.)
1957	4,084	1,485	0.103
1958	4,818	1,494	0.125
1959	5,931	2,597	0.196
1960	6,675	3,782	0.283
1961	7,200	4,865	0.372
1962	8,239	5,657	0.453
1963	9,535	6,226	0.523
1964	10,822	6,796	0.578
1965	11,063	7,789	0.640
1970	15,593	14,200	0.982
1971	18,180	16,440	1.120
1972	21,467	18,980	1.329
1973	24,742	24,027	1.586
1974	30,561	28,524	1.846
1975	39,585	33,701	2.136
1976	48,739	38,567	2.435
1977	59,867	42,521	2.690
1978	73,770	47,176	2.906
1979	97,105	52,225	3.129
1980	98,370		
1981	173,000		
1982	206,383		

PRODUCTION OF CHEMICAL FERTILIZERS (1952-1982)
(Selected Years)

(Unit: million metric tons)

	Total production	Nitrogenous fertilizers	Including Urea	Including Ammonium bicarbonate	Including Others	Phosphate fertilizers	Potash fertilizers
1952	0.190	0.190					
1957	0.735	0.613				0.122	
1965	8.766	4.940				3.822	0.004
1970	12.310	7.250				5.040	0.020
1973	24.254	14.266				9.962	0.062
1976	28.509	18.184				10.288	0.083
1977	35.807	26.236				9.488	0.083
1978	42.454	36.375	8.354	17.287	10.734	5.696	0.083
1979	52.159	42.002	11.610	20.373	10.019	10.094	0.063
1980	12.320	9.990				2.310	0.020
1981	12.390	9.986				2.510	0.020
1982	12.781	10.219				2.537	0.025

(Figures supplied by Planning Bureau of Ministry of Agriculture)

PRODUCTION OF INSECTICIDES (1952-1982)
(Selected Years)

(Unit: 1,000 metric tons)

	Total insecticide production		Total insecticide production
1952	1.92	1977	457.88
1957	64.72	1978	533.35
1965	192.73	1979	522.83
1970	321.28	1980	53.70
1973	454.28	1981	48.40
1976	388.54	1982	45.70

(Figures supplied by Planning Bureau of Ministry of Agriculture)

AGRICULTURAL MODERNIZATION (1952-1982)
(Selected Years)

(I)

	Area of mechanized farming (million hectares)	Area provided with electrically-operated irrigation (million hectares)
1952	0.136	0.317
1957	2.636	1.202
1958	4.727	
1959	6.154	
1960	7.172	
1961	8.160	5.265
1962	8.284	6.065
1963	10.602	5.474
1964	12.791	6.257
1965	15.579	8.093
1970	18.222	14.992
1971	20.780	16.600
1972	21.900	17.817
1973	26.505	19.782
1974	28.498	21.664
1975	33.200	22.889
1976	34.910	24.228
1977	62.640	24.349
1978	40.670	24.894
1979	42.219	25.320
1980	40.990	25.310
1981	36.470	25.230
1982	35.115	25.145

AGRICULTURAL MODERNIZATION (1952-1982)
(Selected Years)

(II)

	Application of chemical fertilizers (million metric tons)	Power consumption in villages (billion kwh)
1952	0.295	0.5
1957	1.794	1.4
1958	2.708	2.4
1959	2.533	3.8
1960	3.164	6.9
1961	2.242	10.3
1962	3.105	18.1
1963	4.483	24.3
1964	5.363	27.8
1965	8.812	37.1
1966	12.582	
1967	13.628	
1968	10.129	
1969	13.611	
1970	15.351	95.7
1971	18.142	104.5
1972	20.931	132.8
1973	25.553	139.9
1974	24.051	156.1
1975	26.579	183.1
1976	28.850	204.8
1977	31.920	221.9
1978	43.681	253.1
1979	52.476	232.7
1980	58.649	320.8
1981	61.768	369.9
1982	68.123	396.9

AVERAGE PER CAPITA DISTRIBUTION BY BASIC ACCOUNTING UNIT IN RURAL PEOPLE'S COMMUNES (1956-1981)

(Selected Years)

(Unit: RMB yuan)

	Distribution to commune members		Distribution to commune members
1956	43.0	1971	62.9
1957	40.5	1972	61.8
1958	41.4	1973	65.4
1959	37.6	1974	65.8
1960	41.3	1975	63.22
1961	48.1	1976	62.80
1962	46.1	1977	64.98
1963	46.2	1978	74.00
1964	47.5	1979	83.40
1965	52.3	1980	85.93
1970	59.5	1981	101.32

ANNUAL INVESTMENTS IN RURAL CAPITAL
CONSTRUCTION AND RATIOS OF THESE
INVESTMENTS WITHIN TOTAL STATE SPENDING

	Total investments in rural capital construction	Farming	Forestry	Water conservancy	Aquiculture	Meteorology
Absolute amounts (in billion yuan):						
1952	5.83	1.67	0.02	4.11		0.03
1957	11.87	4.26	0.52	7.30		0.06
1962	14.39	5.02	1.08	8.27		0.02
1965	24.97	7.38	1.93	15.15	0.46	0.05
1975	38.40	8.55	2.14	25.66	1.70	0.29
1979	57.92	6.14	3.62	34.96	2.82	0.52
1982	34.1	12.74	3.25	17.74		0.39
Proportion (%):						
1952	13.3	3.8		9.4		0.1
1957	8.6	3.1	0.2	5.3		
1962	21.3	7.4	1.6	12.2		
1965	14.6	4.3	1.1	8.9	0.3	
1975	9.8	0.7	0.5	6.6	0.4	0.1
1979	11.6	1.2	0.7	7.0	0.6	0.1

PEASANTS' AVERAGE PER CAPITA CONSUMPTION OF PRINCIPAL FOODSTUFFS IN DIFFERENT LOCALITIES IN 1982

(I)

(Unit: kilogram)

	Grain (unprocessed)	Rice	Wheat	Vegetables
All China	259.97	132.82	59.02	132.04
Beijing	256.11	37.10	139.15	215.17
Tianjin	218.25	41.04	88.95	92.14
Hebei	206.36	5.74	64.68	117.40
Shanxi	236.99	2.02	73.35	91.43
Inner Mongolia	247.42	4.40	82.28	118.82
Liaoning	241.80	40.82	16.39	214.35
Jilin	277.64	42.91	10.97	240.11
Heilongjiang	250.47	26.63	77.86	146.05
Shanghai	276.82	249.60	16.41	117.43
Jiangsu	298.83	187.21	64.87	122.56
Zhejiang	302.12	243.98	23.30	143.37
Anhui	298.42	169.14	101.31	113.25
Fujian	284.23	266.21	2.63	130.79
Jiangxi	319.91	310.65	1.77	166.19
Shandong	216.28	1.98	80.59	118.24
Henan	227.43	27.23	134.09	109.60
Hubei	303.06	228.99	40.62	184.58
Hunan	317.38	300.39	4.20	166.63
Guangdong	274.21	259.82	1.44	121.36
Guangxi	263.93	234.83	0.67	134.34
Sichuan	258.90	156.92	45.42	154.45
Guizhou	222.82	152.26	12.13	142.94
Yunnan	229.78	138.25	18.47	151.70
Shaanxi	246.60	19.03	127.09	68.27
Gansu	223.29	4.47	149.39	35.27
Qinghai	249.04	0.22	171.62	76.49
Ningxia	250.61	62.74	133.40	101.92
Xinjiang	215.80	4.57	138.39	79.23

PEASANTS' AVERAGE PER CAPITA CONSUMPTION
OF PRINCIPAL FOODSTUFFS IN DIFFERENT
LOCALITIES IN 1982

(II)

(Unit: kilogram)

	Vermicelli and noodles made from bean starch and other bean products	Vegetable oil	Animal fat	Pork
All China	2.20	2.07	1.36	8.36
Beijing	0.80	1.51	2.64	8.30
Tianjin	1.02	1.62	1.29	5.68
Hebei	2.44	1.19	0.76	4.87
Shanxi	3.07	1.66	0.52	3.01
Inner Mongolia	3.07	1.85	1.81	11.82
Liaoning	1.96	1.44	2.42	10.61
Jilin	2.62	1.52	1.18	10.49
Heilongjiang	2.69	3.28	1.16	7.75
Shanghai	2.10	4.13	0.48	16.42
Jiangsu	2.85	3.57	0.50	8.17
Zhejiang	2.22	2.10	0.70	11.10
Anhui	5.45	2.98	1.96	7.65
Fujian	2.72	0.61	1.63	7.11
Jiangxi	2.30	2.84	1.24	7.55
Shandong	3.47	2.88	0.68	4.83
Henan	2.76	1.40	0.58	4.33
Hubei	2.04	3.36	1.32	8.69
Hunan	2.66	2.63	2.83	13.10
Guangdong	2.06	2.19	0.93	9.40
Guangxi	0.45	1.12	1.96	8.33
Sichuan	0.64	1.27	1.92	14.64
Guizhou	2.06	0.89	2.23	12.14
Yunnan	1.40	0.52	1.69	10.17
Shaanxi	1.71	1.47	0.77	5.10
Gansu	0.67	1.52	1.29	4.53
Qinghai	0.33	3.87	0.15	8.18
Ningxia	0.91	3.16	0.82	4.56
Xinjiang	0.53	2.70	0.99	1.91

PEASANTS' AVERAGE PER CAPITA CONSUMPTION OF PRINCIPAL FOODSTUFFS IN DIFFERENT LOCALITIES IN 1982

(III)

(Unit: kilogram)

	Beef and mutton	Poultry	Eggs	Fish and shrimp
All China	0.69	0.78	1.42	1.31
Beijing	0.51	0.28	2.69	1.15
Tianjin	1.01	0.20	1.86	2.93
Hebei	0.36	0.08	1.14	0.29
Shanxi	1.09	0.05	1.05	0.04
Inner Mongolia	1.68	0.12	1.33	0.13
Liaoning	0.32	0.30	2.92	1.70
Jilin	0.21	0.71	2.51	0.87
Heilongjiang	0.20	0.32	2.29	0.59
Shanghai	0.40	1.21	4.17	5.59
Jiangsu	0.13	0.97	2.37	2.36
Zhejiang	0.17	1.40	2.41	5.73
Anhui	0.46	1.49	1.71	1.59
Fujian	0.26	1.42	1.13	4.11
Jiangxi	0.13	0.91	1.23	1.65
Shandong	0.48	0.38	2.18	1.12
Henan	0.31	0.26	1.55	0.21
Hubei	0.21	0.62	1.89	2.04
Hunan	0.18	1.50	1.56	1.55
Guangdong	0.14	2.65	0.89	6.15
Guangxi	0.14	1.97	0.45	0.85
Sichuan	0.31	0.64	1.32	0.18
Guizhou	0.18	0.44	0.56	0.26
Yunnan	0.32	0.88	0.73	0.26
Shaanxi	0.22	0.10	0.61	0.01
Gansu	3.08	0.07	0.40	
Qinghai	0.44	0.05	0.66	0.01
Ningxia	2.52	0.19	0.65	0.04
Xinjiang	12.53	0.20	0.53	0.06

PEASANTS' AVERAGE PER CAPITA CONSUMPTION OF PRINCIPAL FOODSTUFFS IN DIFFERENT LOCALITIES IN 1982

(IV)

(Unit: kilogram)

	Sugar	Cigarettes (package of 20)	Wine	Tea
All China	1.18	18.87	2.73	0.21
Beijing	1.39	17.75	3.92	0.68
Tianjin	1.36	17.00	2.24	0.10
Hebei	0.48	13.61	1.07	0.07
Shanxi	0.56	19.44	0.58	0.10
Inner Mongolia	0.63	10.97	1.45	0.21
Liaoning	0.62	5.48	2.32	0.05
Jilin	0.51	3.09	2.60	0.08
Heilongjiang	0.81	4.14	2.12	0.05
Shanghai	3.26	50.15	5.48	0.15
Jiangsu	1.28	26.79	2.80	0.04
Zhejiang	2.56	33.98	8.25	0.22
Anhui	1.40	36.80	2.63	0.24
Fujian	2.69	19.20	5.83	0.28
Jiangxi	1.08	18.53	3.70	0.17
Shandong	0.80	25.87	2.84	0.24
Henan	0.77	22.96	0.89	0.01
Hubei	1.14	32.67	2.97	0.16
Hunan	1.26	24.57	4.52	0.27
Guangdong	4.38	19.20	2.04	0.24
Guangxi	0.94	9.72	3.60	0.02
Sichuan	1.10	16.34	2.90	0.17
Guizhou	0.92	14.49	4.92	0.22
Yunnan	1.53	7.77	2.89	0.28
Shaanxi	0.51	13.33	1.95	0.21
Gansu	0.39	7.25	0.44	0.48
Qinghai	0.17	9.17	0.96	1.13
Ningxia	0.83	14.78	0.40	0.37
Xinjiang	0.83	2.18	0.78	1.41

POSSESSION OF DURABLE GOODS IN DIFFERENT LOCALITIES AT END OF 1982

(Per 100 persons)

(I)

	Bicyles	Sewing machines	Radios	Clocks and watches
All China	9.43	6.00	9.24	19.11
Beijing	30.44	11.66	20.98	52.07
Tianjin	25.00	11.78	18.07	41.68
Hebei	18.31	9.82	15.26	23.95
Shanxi	14.54	10.77	9.55	22.77
Inner Mongolia	13.38	10.45	11.51	20.67
Liaoning	16.88	11.55	14.79	38.67
Jilin	9.81	9.51	15.15	29.50
Heilongjiang	9.78	9.92	14.03	25.99
Shanghai	22.13	14.02	13.62	58.14
Jiangsu	11.25	4.69	11.47	28.07
Zhejiang	7.02	6.39	5.34	36.22
Anhui	5.00	3.90	10.78	11.71
Fujian	3.30	6.04	5.66	26.69
Jiangxi	2.91	1.80	8.52	16.52
Shandong	18.78	7.80	14.09	21.35
Henan	9.65	7.50	11.64	10.44
Hubei	4.36	3.99	8.48	12.39
Hunan	2.99	2.99	4.60	15.20
Guangdong	15.90	8.60	9.94	33.13
Guangxi	12.00	6.00	4.00	15.00
Sichuan	2.71	1.50	5.73	13.30
Guizhou	1.32	2.16	1.96	8.09
Yunnan	2.56	2.29	3.94	8.71
Shaanxi	8.19	6.61	8.64	10.45
Gansu	7.32	4.77	5.21	10.95
Qinghai	5.63	5.18	4.28	9.57
Ningxia	15.37	7.57	9.63	17.52
Xinjiang	8.76	8.80	8.49	14.70

POSSESSION OF DURABLE GOODS IN DIFFERENT LOCALITIES AT END OF 1982
(Per 100 persons)

(II)

	Wrist watches	Television sets	Tape recorders	Electric fans
All China	12.54	0.31	0.12	0.42
Beijing	34.97	6.87	0.44	1.94
Tianjin	23.70	3.48		1.10
Hebei	11.72	0.15	0.03	0.04
Shanxi	13.58	0.10		
Inner Mongolia	11.86	0.16	0.08	
Liaoning	22.03	1.89	0.24	0.08
Jilin	16.75			
Heilongjiang	17.22	0.14	0.08	0.03
Shanghai	41.73	3.06	0.40	4.58
Jiangsu	19.24	0.10	0.02	0.29
Zhejiang	24.91	0.16	0.04	1.29
Anhui	8.45	0.04		0.24
Fujian	18.91	0.08	0.15	0.46
Jiangxi	11.57		0.03	0.13
Shandong	11.85	0.10	0.01	0.03
Henan	7.16	0.02	0.02	
Hubei	9.84	0.04	0.04	0.11
Hunan	12.42	0.04	0.01	0.11
Guangdong	22.18	0.77	1.34	4.91
Guangxi	10.00	0.10	0.10	0.47
Sichuan	9.32	0.13	0.09	0.05
Guizhou	6.41	0.07	0.11	0.02
Yunnan	7.19	0.08	0.25	
Shaanxi	5.82	0.06	0.02	0.02
Gansu	6.27	0.04	0.04	
Qinghai	5.07			
Ningxia	12.95	0.69	0.02	
Xinjiang	10.10	0.20	0.24	

BANK SAVINGS IN VILLAGES IN DIFFERENT
LOCALITIES AT END OF 1981

	Savings in villages (billion yuan)	Savings in towns (billion yuan)	Savings of commune members (billion yuan)	Increase compared with end of 1980 (%)	Average savings per capita (yuan)	Net increase compared with end of 1980 (yuan)
All China	21.169	4.222	16.947	41.9	25.85	7.63
Beijing	0.312	0.147	0.165	38.1	83.16	22.92
Tianjin	0.157	0.025	0.132	48.6	43.99	14.39
Hebei	1.455	0.134	1.321	51.4	31.96	10.85
Shanxi	0.737	0.017	0.720	39.9	36.18	10.31
Inner Mongolia	0.286	0.031	0.255	48.5	20.68	6.76
Liaoning	0.988	0.045	0.943	48.0	43.92	13.23
Jilin	0.414	0.005	0.409	56.2	27.82	10.00
Heilongjiang	0.828	0.232	0.596	45.9	41.16	12.94
Shanghai	0.428	0.088	0.340	21.5	96.42	17.06
Jiangsu	1.492	0.634	0.858	36.0	29.34	7.76

Zhejiang	1.087	0.251	0.836	28.1	32.49	7.12
Anhui	0.556	0.074	0.482	57.6	12.82	4.68
Fujian	0.709	0.242	0.467	42.1	32.96	9.77
Jiangxi	0.460	0.130	0.330	42.1	16.64	4.94
Shandong	2.478	0.038	2.440	36.5	37.52	10.03
Henan	1.342	0.206	1.136	48.8	20.31	6.66
Hubei	0.732	0.114	0.618	38.9	18.59	6.20
Hunan	0.699	0.146	0.553	47.4	15.01	4.83
Guangdong	2.515	0.400	2.115	49.3	52.57	17.36
Guangxi	0.430	0.146	0.284	37.2	13.68	3.71
Sichuan	1.094	0.269	0.825	37.0	12.69	3.43
Guizhou	0.163	0.047	0.116	58.5	6.65	2.45
Yunnan	0.322	0.121	0.201	49.2	11.37	3.75
Tibet	0.014	—	0.014	—	8.80	—
Shaanxi	0.568	0.160	0.408	34.5	23.76	6.09
Gansu	0.191	0.055	0.136	30.9	11.60	2.74
Qinghai	0.063	0.031	0.032	33.8	22.58	5.71
Ningxia	0.064	0.020	0.044	36.0	20.99	5.55
Xinjiang	0.585	0.414	0.171	37.1	64.25	17.38

NEW HOUSING BUILT BY PEASANTS IN DIFFERENT LOCALITIES IN 1982

(Per capita)

(Unit: sq. meter)

	Area of housing built within the year	Area of living quarters at year-end
All China	0.86	10.77
Beijing	1.92	11.98
Tianjin	1.09	9.76
Hebei	0.99	11.36
Shanxi	0.62	10.26
Inner Mongolia	0.67	7.66
Liaoning	0.62	10.87
Jilin	0.44	9.23
Heilongjiang	0.41	7.91
Shanghai	3.35	17.97
Jiangsu	1.30	11.41
Zhejiang	1.73	14.69
Anhui	0.81	10.21
Fujian	0.83	7.67
Jiangxi	0.81	11.57
Shandong	1.04	10.64
Henan	0.82	9.72
Hubei	0.95	14.27
Hunan	1.15	12.89
Guangdong	0.81	11.79
Guangxi	0.58	10.78
Sichuan	0.78	10.94
Guizhou	0.69	10.83
Yunnan	0.57	9.45
Shaanxi	0.61	8.59
Gansu	0.86	10.68
Qinghai	0.47	6.24
Ningxia	0.53	8.58
Xinjiang	0.30	7.83

INDEX

213

中国农村的经济变革

罗涵先　编著

*

新世界出版社出版（北京）

外文印刷厂印刷

中国国际图书贸易总公司发行

（中国国际书店）

北京399信箱

1985年　　第一版

编号：（英）17223—150

00360（精）

00250（平）

17—E—1724